THE NEW SOCIAL WORK

EMPLOYMENT AND EDUCATIONAL SERVICES
IN THE MOBILIZATION FOR YOUTH EXPERIENCE

Employment and Educationa

Services in the Mobilization
for Youth Experience

EDITED BY HAROLD H. WEISSMAN

ASSOCIATION PRESS   NEW YORK

EMPLOYMENT AND EDUCATIONAL SERVICES
IN THE MOBILIZATION FOR YOUTH EXPERIENCE

SBN: Hardbound edition 8096-1728-5

Paperback edition   8096-1733-1
Library of Congress catalog card number: 69-18845

PRINTED IN THE UNITED STATES OF AMERICA

TO
WINSLOW CARLTON
Chairman of the Board
Mobilization For Youth

For Dedication and Devotion
to the Objectives of
the Program

Preface

At its founding, there were several program aspects which distinguished Mobilization For Youth from other social agencies. One was that Mobilization allocated a sizable portion of its resources to research. Yet even with these substantial resources, research could not concern itself with all of the agency's programs. Decisions as to priorities were based on the projected effectiveness of various programs, their relation to the theory which provided the foundation for the overall project, and whether the programs could conform to the rigors of research methodology without compromising either their quality or purpose.

Some programs were researched in great detail, others only in relation to specific aspects, and some unfortunately had to be left uninvestigated.[1] By early 1965, it was clear that much of the experience of the agency would be lost unless it was systematically described and analyzed.

Of particular concern was the practice knowledge that had been gained—the reservoir of insights, ideas, experiences, and judgments about the range of interaction and interventions staff were involved in, the structures and mechanisms they had devised, and the results achieved through their efforts.

To codify and refine this practice knowledge, MFY applied for a grant from the Office of Juvenile Delinquency and Youth Development of the Department of Health, Education and Welfare. Grant No. 67224, effective July 1, 1966, through June 30, 1968, provided for a Program Reporting Department consisting of a

[1] A list of the research studies and reports about Mobilization programs is appended to Vol. 4, *Justice and the Law*, as well as an epilogue and a discussion of the administration of the total MFY program.

staff of writers and program analysts. According to the grant's stipulations, the department was to . . .

> . . . tell the story of each program division from its beginning, inserting at the appropriate places changes or new emphases divergent from those originally conceived, problems which emerged during the course of the program and how they were dealt with, techniques and methods which were used successfully and unsuccessfully, involvement with other MFY programs, participation statistics as well as any other pertinent statistical information. It will also include descriptions of program accomplishments, and other useful information relating to aspects of the program such as training and hiring of staff, administration and supervision. The intention . . . is to provide people who have participated in a unique social adventure with an opportunity to develop their own ideas and practice insights and to exchange them with others similarly engaged.

A few of the papers which appear in this book and the other volumes in this collection were written by line staff members of the particular divisions; most were written by the Program Reporting staff; some are an amalgam of the work of both line staff and Program Reporting staff. A member of the Program Reporting staff was assigned responsibility for the reports on each of the program divisions of Mobilization. This responsibility included gathering all prior reports and published material of the division, developing with line staff an outline for the projected volume, observing the operation of programs, preparing working drafts— alone or in conjunction with line staff—and discussing these with all staff involved with the topic being covered.

All the papers in this volume went through several drafts; many were substantially altered, some were combined, and some, after discussion with the staff, were deleted. In addition, former executives of the agency—particularly Dr. Richard Cloward, director of research, Dr. Melvin Herman, director of the Division of Employment Opportunities, Herbert Goldsmith, director of the Division of Educational Opportunities, and Hannah Levin, assistant director of the Division of Educational Opportunities—gave their comments and suggestions. Their help was invaluable in ensuring the accuracy and quality of the material presented.

As editor of this volume, it was my responsibility to make final decisions as to what material should be included, what should be emphasized, and what value should be accorded various conflicting ideas and sentiments. In this process it was necessary for me to rework many of the papers done by others in the interest of economy of time and effort. Any bias or error which has thus inadvertently crept in remains my responsibility.

There are a great many able people to whom considerable credit is due; foremost is Bertram M. Beck, executive director of Mobilization since 1965. He first conceived the idea for these volumes and was instrumental in obtaining the grant that made them possible. Special note must be made of the time and effort which the Employment and Educational Services staffs gave to the preparation of this volume. Dr. Martin Moed, a former director, and Irwin Feifer, current director of the Division of Employment Opportunities, were particularly helpful. Elmira Hull, Edwin Friend, Evelyn Kay, Raymond Berger, Richard Tobias, Jerome Schenkman, Maria Sein, Eddie Jones, David Dennis, and Anita Vogel read individual papers and made helpful comments.

Burton Weinstein of the Program Reporting staff coordinated the writing of papers for the Division of Employment Opportunities. Fred Lorber made substantial contributions to each of the employment papers. Ruth Dropkin read the education papers and made useful editorial suggestions. Welton Smith gathered much of the data upon which the education papers were based.

Danielle Spellman, Nancy Dannenberg, and Martha King typed and retyped the papers, not without complaint but always with humor and concern. Each of them also, when the need arose, assisted in observing programs and was a helpful critic of the papers.

Beverly Luther served as my assistant in this project. Without her help it could not have been brought to a conclusion. She relieved me of a variety of administrative duties and faultlessly followed through with innumerable details. Gladys Topkis edited the papers, as she has done with so much of the written material produced at Mobilization. A considerable portion of the credit for the style and clarity of the material goes to her.

Each of the sections in this book and the other three volumes— *Individual and Group Services, Community Development, Justice*

and the Law—begins with a statement of the ideas and concepts
the workers intended to apply in a particular program division.
The individual papers which make up each volume describe what
happened when these ideas were put into effect and what was
learned from the experience. Some of the papers deal with the
history of a specific program, some deal with broad issues and
concerns in social work and other professions, and others describe
experiences in many programs. The concluding chapter in each
section summarizes the major issues which emerged from the experiences described.

The four volumes are meant to constitute an intellectual history
of a project which in all likelihood represents a watershed in the
development of social welfare in America. This type of history
perforce emphasizes learning. It does not tell the comprehensive
history of the agency. It may even dwell more on failures than
prudent public relations would dictate. The volumes, as such, are
not intended to provide a balanced picture of the agency. They
are intended, rather, to give readers an opportunity to share the
insights, ideas, experiences, and judgments of those who shaped
and were shaped by it.

—H. H. W.

Contents

Introduction

The slum is, in its least complex form, a disorderly mechanism for human destruction, operating through crumbling houses and relatively unconnected inhabitants in a loosely defined geographic area. At its most developed, it is a homeland for a particular minority group or assemblage of groups, a neighborhood with its own traditions, where a foreign language may be the common tongue and where the accepted customs, loyalties, and hostilities may be divergent from, or even directly opposed to, those of society outside. New York City encompasses a wide assortment of slums, of all sizes and conditions, in all stages of development and disorder. Among them, Manhattan's Lower East Side has the longest history as a slum neighborhood, although the component languages and customs have changed several times through the years and are not uniform today from one group's heartland in the area to another's.

The Lower East Side first became a slum neighborhood thanks very largely to the Irish Potato Famine of 1846, which drove the impoverished "wild geese" abroad as mercenaries and refugees. Irish immigrants began to pour into America in the 1840's and 1850's. New York received a larger number than any other city, and several parts of the Lower East Side became Irish homelands, especially the Five Points area, where a small Irish enclave still exists, and the area along the East River, where many Irish were employed on the docks. The zone near the Bowery became a drinking and red-light district. Like later minority groups who felt themselves isolated by poverty in the middle of the New Paradise they had come to find, the Irish formed gangs. The famous Bowery Gangs included both adults and adolescents and controlled their "turf" with savagery. And, as was true of later delinquent and gangster groups, the Irish proved to be useful to the powers-that-be —in this case Tammany Hall—who found employment for the Irish Bowery Gangs during elections, and a value in the Irish vote.

Then the Irish took over Tammany Hall and became American, through the acquisition of political power and the process of acculturation. They were fortunate in that this process for them did not involve learning a foreign language or accepting a basically alien culture. In the eyes of some of the groups that succeeded them on the Lower East Side, the image of the American was that of the Irishman.

The Germans began arriving in the 1860's and 1870's and became for a time the most numerous immigrant group in the city. In the 1860's it was estimated that two thirds of the 120,000 German-born residents of New York City lived on the Lower East Side in an area which the immigrants called *Kleindeutschland,* or *Deutschlandle.* Many of the Irish moved away, and the beer halls and delicatessens of Germany were duplicated on the streets of the Lower East Side.

This German Lower East Side seems to have been a comparatively peaceful slum. Many of the immigrants were artisans. There were fewer peasants than among the Irish, and big city living, in their recreated Germany, seems to have come fairly easily to them. The Germans, even given the handicap of their foreign language, were a group whose customs, tastes, and personal appearance did not militate against their relatively undramatic integration into American society.

This was not the case with the next two immigrant groups to arrive in the Lower East Side. The eastern European Jews and the primarily southern Italians who came in hordes toward the end of the nineteenth century were foreign in their customs, looks, and language, with a tendency to shout and laugh in public too loudly for the taste of traditional America, surrounded with the aura of sensuality and depravity with which lighter-skinned races have always tended to endow those darker than themselves.

The center of Little Italy lay west of the Lower East Side, but the Italian population extended well into the area. The immigrants were almost all peasants or else refugees from the hideous slums of Naples and Palermo and Agrigento. They came to America in swaying ships packed with hundreds of their fellows, and were met by waiting relatives who took them to the tenements that would be their new homes. The tubs of family washing and the piles of sewing to be done on a piecework basis might already be prepared for the girl, the address of the gang-labor contractor and his assurances of "plenty of work for a boy from the old hometown" welcomed the man. They constructed their Little Italy as well as they could, but for a Sicilian peasant, the sidewalks of New York buried in snow differed in more than geography and climate from the sun-baked, rocky farmlands of Sicily. The southern Italian came from a region of feudal landlords who were still called barons, an intensely traditional and immovable society; in America everything seemed in flux and up for grabs, provided that one was ruthless or knowledgeable enough. Those who were not struggled along; those who were rose out of areas like the Lower East Side into the goods and benefits of middle-class American living, through the routes of business, politics, dogged and desperate acquisition of a professional education, or crime. For some there was a bitter price to be paid in renunciation, in self-hatred for the foreignness which the parents had given and the child still, in spite of himself, retained. American acceptability often came at a profound psychological cost.

The eastern European Jews were the group that most characterized the Lower East Side in the first half of the twentieth century. In New York, in the nation at large, and outside America, the Lower East Side came to mean the Jewish ghetto. By 1900, the East Side was already the largest, most densely populated Jewish community in the world. Of two million Jewish immigrants in America at the time of World War I, three quarters had lived for a time on the Lower East Side. Although there remained scattered pockets of other ethnic groups—Italians, a handful of Germans, small neighborhoods of Irish, an enclave of Slavonic people—virtually all of the Lower East Side, from Cherry Street to Tenth Street, from the East River to the Bowery, was considered the ghetto.

The Russian pogroms of the 1880's and 1890's were the propelling force for the Jewish immigration. There had been a settlement of German Jews on the Lower East Side before then, and these now Americanized Germans tended to be ill at ease with their alien co-religionists, condescending and superior. Some of them owned the garment businesses in which the new arrivals were employed. Other German Jews were active in philanthropy and in attempts to Americanize the immigrants.

The East European Jews themselves were divided into groups who spoke different dialects of Yiddish and had somewhat different customs. Russians, Lithuanians, Poles, Galicians, and Romanians tended to settle among their own and preserve their own cultural variants, but they could easily understand each other's Yiddish. The Lower East Side became a center of Yiddish culture, with a developed literature, an extremely active theater, and six flourishing newspapers, including the still existing *Daily Forward*. In its time, the *Forward* was an important Socialist newspaper, in the forefront of the Jewish labor movement during the days of the early unions and the violent strikes.

The Jewish East Side has become known, through the writings of nostalgic former residents, as a foreign enclave, with foods and sounds and colors and customs that marked it apart from the larger society. It was that, of course, but it was also a tenement slum where the measure of success was departure, where the young members of street gangs fought and developed into full-time hoodlums struggling with the Irish and Italian gangsters for the vast spoils of Prohibition.

America's first settlement house, the University Settlement, was founded on the Lower East Side in the 1880's. The settlement movement on the Lower East Side pioneered in attempts to deal with the problems of slums, such as campaigns for increased recreational facilities, housing reform, and child-labor legislation.

In the 1930's and 1940's the ghetto began to break up. Many Jews moved to the Bronx and Brooklyn, leaving behind the old, the economically trapped, and the failures. In the next two decades another group of immigrants arrived to change once again the complexion and language of the Lower East Side. Puerto Ricans have come in vast numbers from the slums of Ponce and San Juan and New York's East Harlem, joined by lesser numbers of Negroes from the American South or from New York's Harlem or Bedford-Stuyvesant. The combined Negro and Puerto Rican population of New York City increased 250 percent between 1925 and 1950. A small colony of Puerto Rican cigarmakers had lived on Cherry Street in the Lower East Side since the 1920's, but the major destination of the postwar Puerto Rican immigration to New York City was "El Barrio," East Harlem centering around Third Avenue and 101st Street. The Negroes coming up from the South and the West Indies went first to Harlem and later to Bedford-Stuyvesant, which were long-established Negro ghettos. Therefore, for the Puerto Ricans and Negroes who began moving down to the Lower East Side in the 1940's and 1950's as the Jewish population vacated the tenements, the Lower East Side was not a primary area of settlement, a homeland, as it had been for the Germans and the Jews, but a spillover area without structure or traditions.

Many of the tenement streets awaiting the newcomers were little different from what they had been fifty or sixty years before, but the postwar building boom had swept some of the others away. Low-income public-housing projects and middle-income cooperatives have been built on the Lower East Side. The cooperatives have brought the middle class into the neighborhood for the first time in a century, to join the low-income Puerto Ricans and Negroes who live in the tenements and public housing projects. The residents of the cooperatives are generally middle class or so-called stable working class whites, primarily Jewish. In the tenements east of Avenue B, the western boundary of the Mobilization For Youth project, almost none of the previous white residents remain. In recent years, increasing though still relatively small numbers of a different kind of slum dweller have arrived: artists and those who attach themselves to artistic communities, drawn by the low rents growing less and less available in Greenwich Village. In the parlance of renting agents, the Lower East Side is now the East Village, as a result of this movement and in the attempt to capitalize on it.

The section of the Lower East Side which Mobilization For Youth singled out as its target area is primarily a Puerto Rican slum. Some Italians still live in the southern portion, a small Slavonic group to the north, a number of Chinese on certain streets who are moving over from Chinatown to the west. Jews still own much of the housing and many of the businesses, and there are old-fashioned outdoor Jewish markets on Orchard Street and on Avenue C. From a survey of the Mobilization area taken in 1961, it was estimated that 27 percent of the population was Jewish, most of them residents of the cooperatives. But the basically Puerto Rican nature of the area is very evident from the record shops and bodegas and botanicas and the bongos out on the street at the first touch of spring.

The postwar wave of Puerto Rican immigration now seems to be nearing its end. The Puerto Ricans came, as citizens of the United States, for the economic opportunities which were wanting in Puerto Rico, and they stayed because, even in the rat-ridden tenements of El Barrio, things really were somewhat better here, or at least more promising.

New York offered many of the Puerto Ricans their first confrontation with direct racial prejudice. The pecking order of the oppressed tended to establish itself again as in America it usually, sadly has. A certain degree of hostility developed between Negroes and Puerto Ricans since they were competing for the same bottom-of-the-heap jobs and some of the same slum housing, and, less materially, because the bottom of society is a very narrow place for people to share. Recognizable Negro–Puerto Ricans, a minority among the immigrants, were in a very difficult position: On the one hand they had to deal with a double load of prejudice; on the other, many of them came to feel that being Spanish and black was somehow better than being simply an American Negro, and so they clung even more tenaciously to their language and denied all connection with the American black man. On occasion, as occurred in the process of rent-strike organizing activities on the Lower East Side, light-skinned Puerto Ricans have been told they were "more American" than the darker-skinned Hispanicos and used as a shock force against their own people.

Gradually that section of the Lower East Side which forms the Mobilization For Youth project area is becoming the kind of slum one can call a neighborhood. The Puerto Rican has come to feel at home in the Lower East Side, and the area has become a zone of "Spanish color." But even a slum that is a neighborhood continued to be a machine for human destruction. The difficulties with school that usually burden lower-class youngsters are multiplied for children whose native language is Spanish and whose cultural values are Caribbean. During the late 1950's, the "heroic era" of teenage gang warfare in New York City, some of the casualties took place on the Lower East Side where bopping gangs formed by kids of Puerto Rican, Italian and Negro descent fought with adult weapons for control of their respective turf. With the decline of the conflict gangs, and in part a reason for the decline, came a huge increase in heroin addiction throughout New York. The junkie on the nod as the result of a shot of horse became an everyday sight on the Lower East Side. And many of the junkies were adolescents, copping out young on the consumer's society that seemed to have very little in the way of possible consumption to offer them.

Along with the increase in addiction came an upsurge in petty theft. Slum dwellers are always the first to suffer from those among them who choose criminal activity. This pattern of declining gang conflict and rising heroin addiction and petty crime characterized juvenile delinquency on the Lower East Side when, in 1962, Mobilization For Youth actively undertook to "mount . . . a major demonstration program to attack the problem of juvenile delinquency" by "expanding opportunities for conventional behavior."

Mobilization For Youth had its inception at a meeting of the board of directors of the Henry Street Settlement in June 1957, where a report was read on the growth of delinquency on the Lower East Side. In the Mobilization area this rate grew from 28.7 offenses per 1,000 youths in 1951 to 62.8 per 1,000 in 1960. Appalled by the dimensions of the problem, the board proposed that research begin immediately on a program of massive response to the increasing rate of juvenile delinquency. A planning process began which took four and a half years to complete. During a preliminary stage, faculty members of the Columbia University School of Social Work, assisted by a grant from the Taconic Foundation, conducted research emphasizing the existing youth-serving agencies on the Lower East Side and what could be learned from them in terms of practice. In a second stage of research, beginning in November 1959 and made possible by grants from the National Institute of Mental Health, a unifying principle of expanding opportunities was worked out as a direct basis for action. This principle was drawn from the concepts outlined by sociologists Richard Cloward and Lloyd Ohlin in their book *Delinquency and Opportunity*. Drs. Cloward and Ohlin regarded delinquency as the result of the disparity perceived by low-income youths between their legitimate aspirations and the opportunities—social, economic, political, educational—made available to them by society. If the gap between opportunity and aspiration could be bridged, they believed delinquency would be reduced; that would be the agency's goal.

The geographical boundaries set for Mobilization coincided with the zone of greatest poverty and highest delinquency on the Lower East Side: Avenue B on the west, the East River on the east, East 14th Street to the north and the City Hall junction to the south running into a tip of Lower Manhattan. The area had a population in 1961 of approximately 107,000, of whom 27 percent were Jewish, 11 percent Italian, 25 percent "other white," 8 percent Negro, 3 percent Oriental, and 26 percent Puerto Rican. These percentages do not reflect the ethnic groups served by Mobilization, however, for a considerable number of the whites, as we have noted, were financially stable, with little need for Mobilization services. The youth population was 90 percent Puerto Rican and Negro. And the percentage of Puerto Rican and Negro residents almost doubled between 1960 and 1967.

More than half of the tenement housing (62.4 percent) was classified as substandard by the 1960 census. Although the citywide unemployment rate in that year was 5.0 percent, some ninety neighborhoods (half of them in Manhattan) had rates at least twice the citywide figure. The Lower East Side contained one third of Manhattan's double-rate neighborhoods. Forty-one percent of its households received some form of financial assistance, and 37 percent of its adult residents had failed to complete the eighth grade.

A thirty-three-man board of directors was established for Mobilization, including eleven faculty members from the Columbia School of Social Work and leaders of various citywide and national agencies, such as the Office of the Commonwealth of Puerto Rico, the New York Community Service Society, and the Urban League. Major funding came from the City of New York, the National Institute of Mental Health, the Ford Foundation, and the President's Committee on Juvenile Delinquency.

Supplied with these resources and armed with its extensive background of preparation and research, Mobilization For Youth began its service projects in 1962, with an initial staff of approximately three hundred.

Besides a Division of Research, programs were grouped under four major divisions: Educational Services, Employment Services, Services to Individuals and Families, and Community Development. This latter division included Services to Groups. In 1964 a fifth division, Legal Services, was added.

The project from the first attracted much local and national attention because of the experimental nature of its programs and the prospect that, should Mobilization's modes of dealing with the problem of juvenile delinquency prove successful, similar programs might be mounted throughout the country. Many of the staff members were highly trained specialists; others were local residents who had had experience in community work; nearly all began their work with a high degree of commitment and enthusiasm. What follows is a record of their effort.

Henry Heifetz

PART I

Employment Opportunities

1

Overview of Employment Opportunities

Harold H. Weissman

Providing youth with employment opportunities was one of the major means by which Mobilization hoped to combat delinquency on the Lower East Side, for occupation is generally regarded as the chief determinant of social status and the principal road to upward mobility. If low-income youths are not to become delinquent, then they, as well as other youths, must find their connection with society through their work roles.

The employment problem in the Mobilization area seemed immense. When the action program was initiated in 1962, the unemployment rate for Lower East Side youth in the sixteen-to-twenty age group was about 17 percent, as compared with a rate of 7.5 percent for the city as a whole.[1] And if young workers in general had a hard time in the labor market, it was clear that those with poor education and a lack of salable skills had an even more difficult time. Lower-class youths were members of the "last to be hired, first to be fired" category.

Mobilization's employment program had three overriding aims: (1) to increase the employability of lower-class youths by providing them with the skills they need for employment; (2) to increase the number of employment opportunities for lower-class youths by demonstrating to the public at large what these youths can do if they are given a chance; and (3) to increase the visibility for youths of the job opportunities available to them. To achieve these ends,

[1] *A Proposal For the Prevention and Control of Delinquency by Expanding Opportunities,* (New York, Mobilization For Youth, 1961), p. 92.

Mobilization began, in October 1962, the first nonresident training program conducted in an urban ghetto which combined on-the-job training, in-school and out-of-school work training, trade training, apprenticeship training, remedial education, vocational counseling and evaluation, job development, and job placement.

Mobilization's experience with these programs greatly influenced the development of the Neighborhood Youth Corps authorized under the Economic Opportunity Act of 1964. While a number of innovations were made and procedures modified over the years, which will be described in the chapters that follow, the basic structure of the MFY program has remained constant:

1 A youth job center which handles intake, counseling, testing, and placement of youths in training programs and on jobs;

2 Subsidized work experience and training both in training sites located at MFY and at other agencies;

3 On-the-job training with private employers, enrollment in apprenticeship programs, and trade-school training;

4 Remedial education;

5 Part-time jobs for in-school youths in public-service or private nonprofit agencies.

In the main, the work program serves primarily youths, both male and female, sixteen to twenty-one years of age who are out of school and live within the MFY area.[2] Trainees are paid a stipend which ranged over the years from $1 to $1.50 an hour.

At the youth job center, staff attempt to evaluate each applicant's capabilities and help him establish suitable vocational goals. If he is ready for employment or advanced training, he is placed in an apprenticeship or on-the-job training situation or on a job in private industry. If he is deemed unready to compete in the job market, he is provided with subsidized work training. Individual counseling, testing, and remedial education are geared to help trainees progress from beginning to more advanced training and employment. Some twenty different training sites were set up at

[2] Those within the age range, but living out of the area, were offered placement help by staff of the State Employment Service assigned to MFY. Approximately 80 percent of the trainees were school dropouts.

Mobilization, covering a variety of jobs in such areas as food service, hospital aides, sewing, auto mechanics, gas-station service, clerical, furniture repair, carpentry, and building maintenance and repair. Training sites outside of Mobilization For Youth covered jobs in Federal, state, and local agencies, both public and private, such as the Department of Parks, Veterans Administration, Legal Aid Society, etc.

It was anticipated that applicants to the training programs would differ in the skills and aptitudes they possessed. Finding the right training program and/or a job for each applicant was a prime concern of the staff. While the complexity of this task will be described in detail in the papers in this section, a brief profile of the trainee population should serve as a useful introduction.

The Trainees

Perhaps the major problems in matching trainees with programs were the gaps in knowledge about the trainees themselves and certain unanticipated shifts in the trainee population. The program's planners had expected a high demand for jobs and a lack of skill among potential trainees, but they knew little about such matters as the attitude of disadvantaged youths toward work, the occupations they desired and expected, the amount of money they wanted and needed, the influences of the neighborhood, peer groups, and family upon occupational interests and attitudes, and the effects of employer behavior on low-income youth.

From the first day, the agency was dealing with a trainee population considerably different from a group of average adolescents. A report on an early group of trainees revealed that only 20 percent lived with both parents. Twenty-one percent spoke only Spanish, and another 25 percent had only limited knowledge of English. Approximately 30 percent came from families on welfare, and a considerable number of the female applicants were married with at least one child. Financial and family problems were the most commonly given reasons for leaving school (37 percent of those interviewed). About a third indicated a poor adaptation to the school experience—dislike of school, conflict, possibly expulsion. Most trainees said they preferred working to going to school.

Ethnically, the enrollment pattern shifted from 60 percent Puerto Rican in 1962 to 85 percent in 1967. There was a corresponding decline in the enrollment of Negro youths from about 25 percent to 10 percent. The remainder, mostly Caucasian with some Oriental enrollment, varied between 8 and 10 percent. Serving a Puerto Rican majority, many of whom could not speak English well, the program had to have a bilingual reception and intake staff. Predictably the program took on a Puerto Rican image.

Originally largely male, the trainee population shifted to equal numbers of males and females. The age of the average trainee has also shifted from about 18½ years to 17½. Some have speculated that this shift is related to the military draft, the opening up of other types of training programs, or simply exhausting the older age pool. Others point out that older adolescents feel they can do better on their own in view of the low training stipend that is paid. Trainees tended to view Mobilization's work-training crews as actual jobs and the training stipend as a wage. To many youths this was translated into "Mobilization has low-paying jobs, and I can do better on my own."

A major problem for the staff was the difference between what enrollees said and what they tended to do, especially in the younger age brackets. In general, if they were formerly employed, they said they liked their previous jobs and believed promotional opportunities were good. They said they wanted and needed training. Salary was not so important as the opportunity for advancement. When asked if they would accept certain negative working conditions and a low salary in a job that prepared them for advancement, most trainees answered affirmatively. They appeared to feel that a man should work for the morally and socially productive values of work.

In practice, however, many trainees were reluctant to accept a job if they could be fired easily, if the work was dirty or highly competitive, or if the boss was always "on their back." They placed value on jobs in the neighborhood, or high-paying jobs with no future, and often left jobs or training after they had accumulated some pocket money. They tended to attribute unsuccessful employment experiences to external forces or other people.

How to deal with these behaviors was a major concern in every aspect of the employment program. The program efforts are best understood in the context of a trainee work profile. Four groups were identified:

1. *The Severely Disabled.* This group, which comprised about 10 percent of all enrollees, consisted of youths with severe emotional or psychological difficulties, mental deficiences, physical handicaps, and such problems as drug addiction. MFY did not develop special programs for these youths and tried to keep them out of the regular programs. Occasionally, however, addicts or other emotionally disturbed adolescents slipped through the screening process. Counselors and crew chiefs tried to work with them, but the achievements were too limited to warrant the great cost. In addition, these youths generally had a demoralizing and destructive effect on other enrollees.

2. *Those in Need of Prevocational Training.* This group comprised approximately 65 percent of the enrollees. It included those who were considered not ready to compete on the outside job market but with enough ability to enter training. They were generally characterized by immaturity, lack of work skills, and a meager understanding of the demands and responsibilities of entry-level jobs. Differentiation among this group was difficult. Some problems were easy to identify: English-language difficulties, hostile or suspicious attitudes toward counselors and bosses, lack of job-related skills or fundamental work habits such as getting to work on time, taking instruction, responsibility for the property of others, etc. But these problems almost always occurred in combination and were difficult to isolate from one another. Among this group were also many youths who demanded immediate job placement, refusing to work for the relatively small training stipends. Employment counselors daily faced the dilemma of permitting unprepared clients in financial need to go directly into jobs where they risked failure or dead-end employment or to try to motivate them to take training programs at the risk of their rejecting the program completely.

3. *Those Ready for Skill Training.* This group made up approximately 15 percent of the enrollees. Many of them were high-school graduates. They lacked marketable skills but had the self-discipline and interest to pursue specialized skill training.

4. *Those Prepared for Advanced Training or Job Placement*. This group comprised about 10 percent of the enrollees and consisted of those with work experience or high-school diplomas backed with some skills and a great deal of self-confidence.

Issues

Some of the other major problems staff faced besides the meshing of trainee and training should be understood prior to reading the papers that follow. One initial problem was whether the agency saw its primary role as demonstration or as service. A related issue was whether the employment program was to serve just delinquents or all the low-income youths in the neighborhood. An initial emphasis in the Division of Employment Opportunities was to develop innovative employment and work-training services for delinquent-prone youths. This meant that, rather than attempting to train all such youths on the Lower East Side, the agency would seek to demonstrate through its programs why changes should be made in legislation that impeded training programs and in the procedures of existing agencies, such as the Department of Welfare and the Board of Education, which discouraged youths from seeking training.[3] It would also try to influence private industry to hire school dropouts.

The division's attempt to remain a demonstration program was constantly under attack. Soon after its doors opened, the agency was picketed by a group of teen-agers with signs reading: "Do we have to be delinquents to get a job?" With no other similar program available, it was inevitable that the service needs of the neighborhood would demand equal consideration with the demonstration desires of the agency.

Thus a policy conflict developed within the agency over what was to be demonstrated and who was to be the beneficiary of the agency's services. Initially, the division was unable to provide enough training positions for all applicants. Therefore choices had

[3] For a detailed description of its success in this phase of its work, see Melvin Herman and Bernard Rosenberg, "Effecting Organizational Change Through a Demonstration Project: The Case of a Youth Work Program," in George Brager and Francis Purcell, editors, *Community Action Against Poverty* (New Haven, College and University Press, 1967), pp. 119–29.

to be made. The director of the Detached Worker Project [4] argued that delinquents were the chief target of change efforts and that therefore delinquent youths should receive priority in service. The director of employment services argued that almost all of the applicants to the program were either delinquent or delinquent-prone, even if they were not members of street gangs.[5]

Another issue which complicated the attempt to match applicants to training programs was whether their primary needs were for training in specific occupation skills, or in work attitudes and habits. According to one view, the unemployability of these youths could be traced to the youths themselves: They were unable to perform well on a job because of poor work attitudes and habits, limited ability, and totally unrealistic vocational goals. Such youngsters need help, according to this view, in improving their attitudes, in gaining greater self-awareness, and in acquiring some of the fundamental skills needed for getting and holding a job.[6] The alternate approach, that of specific occupational training, assumes that the problem of youth unemployment stems from a lack of the skills needed for specific jobs, coupled with the changing job patterns of the economy. This approach is posited on the fact that there are only a limited number of occupations open to relatively unskilled youth and that the labor supply for these jobs is large enough to saturate whatever openings exist before these youngsters can even get to the gate. In this view, then, it is a market failure rather than some lack in the prospective trainees that accounts for the problem of unemployment among youths. From this point of view, low-income youths need training in occupations which have openings and in which a future shortage of labor can be expected.

When Mobilization's work program opened, the emphasis was

[4] For a description of this program see the chapter on "Group Service Programs and Their Effect on Delinquents" in Vol. 1, *Individual and Group Services.*

[5] The issue was really whether to emphasize the prevention or the treatment of delinquency. This issue was not resolved during the first five years of Mobilization's existence. What occurred in most instances was a compromise. A certain number of job-training slots were allocated to members of street gangs, the majority of openings were maintained for the general population of low-income youth.

[6] *Youth Employment Programs in Perspective* (Washington, D.C., Department of Health, Education and Welfare, 1965), pp. 11–13.

on finding jobs for youngsters and placing them as fast as possible. This was done primarily because the agency wished to demonstrate that, if opportunities were made available, the youngsters could make use of them and also on the assumption that trainees could learn best in work situations. It soon became apparent that most trainees had little idea of what job they wanted to train for. To give trainees some experience in a variety of work areas, a policy was instituted to provide work experiences in a number of employment areas, such as the building trades, an automobile shop, furniture making, etc.

This rotating system of work experience was discontinued after a brief and disappointing trial, but the experiment led to the development of a Vocational Evaluation Unit for assessing the interests and aptitudes of trainees through the use of specially designed work samples. In fact, there weren't enough different types of training sites at Mobilization to test adequately the vocational aptitude of trainees or to give them a wide enough variety of work experiences from which to select an occupation.

A similar problem arose in another area, centering around the relative importance of remedial education in a work-training program.[7] One group of proponents argued that to place low-income youths in jobs without giving them the educational background for advancement and promotion is ultimately to trap them in a cycle of poverty. The other group argued that a majority of youths in MFY's programs were dropouts from school, that, even if the agency wanted to emphasize education, the trainees would reject it, and that the best way to convey to an adolescent that he needs education is through his experience on a job.

Partly in response to concern over many of the policy issues which had been raised, the Employment Division in 1965 decided to design and carry out a research project which, it was hoped, would provide answers to some of the practice dilemmas they had faced during the first years of the division's operation.[8] The re-

[7] For a discussion of the ramifications of this policy issue, see Richard A. Cloward and Robert Ontell, "Our Illusions About Training," *American Child* (January 1965).

[8] At the time of this writing, the data from the experiment have not been analyzed. It is expected that the experiment will be published by the Re-

search project is intended to evaluate the relative effectiveness of three alternate methods of providing vocational services in terms of trainees' subsequent vocational success: (1) training in work crews located within MFY, versus training on sites outside the agency; (2) training on a half-time basis together with half-time remedial education, or full-time work training; and (3) pretraining vocational evaluation, including testing and familiarization with various work areas, or no vocational evaluation before training.

In order to be able to study the operation of any one of the three experimental variables, while at the same time varying the other two—e.g., in order to compare training sites located at MFY and those located outside the agency while varying the educational and vocational evaluation conditions—a 2 x 2 x 2 factorial design, yielding eight subgroups, was used. Registrants at the work center were assigned randomly at reception to various program groups, as dictated by the research design.[9]

The research study is also attempting to determine whether individuals who have participated in a subsidized work-training program subsequently exhibit greater vocational success than nonparticipants. To the extent that this does occur, are the participants' better vocational outcomes attributable to exposure to training or to the fact that they may subsequently receive job-referral and placement assistance not available to nonparticipants?

Close to eleven thousand teenagers and young adults applied for service in the Employment Program during the first five years of its existence. Not all of these applicants entered training, and not all those who entered training were able to complete it and secure a job. The papers that follow describe how the program operated and

---

search Center, Columbia University School of Social Work, in 1969. Its official title is "An Experiment to Test Three Major Issues of Work Program Methodology Within Mobilization For Youth's Integrated Services to Out-of-school Unemployed Youth."

[9] For a discussion of the problems caused by randomization of clients and other difficulties of instituting a research program in an already existing service operation, see Melvin Herman and Michael Munk, *Decision-Making in Poverty Programs: Case Studies from Youth-Work Agencies* (New York, Columbia University Press, 1968), pp. 166–74.

changed over the years. The concluding paper in this section offers
an appraisal of its effectiveness.[10]

[10] The yearly budgets for the division were as follows: 1962–63, $533,-
189.00; 1963–64, $1,356,596.00; 1964–65, $1,265,108.00; 1965–66, $1,365,-
152.00; 1966–67, $1,679,179.00. These budgets do not include indirect costs
—fiscal services, executive offices, central services, occupancy costs, personnel and public relations—which averaged an additional 25 percent a year.
With the passage of the Economic Opportunity Act in 1964, which authorized the Neighborhood Youth Corps, and the start of the experiment in 1965,
the Department of Labor and the Office of Economic Opportunity were the
major funding sources for the program. Before that, the President's Committee on Juvenile Delinquency and the Ford Foundation were the major
sources of funds.

2

The Processing of the Trainee

Fred Lorber

Merely establishing a work-training agency in a low-income community does not guarantee that the most needy youths will avail themselves of its services. The success of such an agency depends largely upon the way in which its program is interpreted by its target population and the techniques it uses to attract and hold disadvantaged youth. Even the preliminary processing can have an important influence on whether a trainee drops out from the program or, if he continues, whether he derives as much benefit as possible from it.

Recruitment

Mobilization has had little trouble in recruiting sizable numbers of trainees. Several recruitment techniques were developed which insured a steady flow of applicants. From its inception, MFY was known in the community as an agency that provides jobs for youth. The publicity attendant upon its opening in 1962 stressed this image and resulted in the agency's immediate inundation by requests for jobs and training. Over the years this picture of MFY was sustained by advertisements in the Spanish press and on the radio, posters, and news coverage, as well as by the general activities of the agency in the community. In the periodic recruitment campaigns, current trainees were often used to recruit new trainees.

In order to extend the agency services to sectors of the community geographically remote from the main program office, branch offices were opened, which resulted in increased recruitment. In addition, an army-surplus radio field truck staffed by employment counselors was used in different sections of the MFY service area every few days. The counselors on the truck would explain the services offered by the program, distribute informative leaflets and referral cards in Spanish and English, and answer pertinent questions. The use of this mobile unit was usually followed by large numbers of applicants coming to the agency within a few days.

The sources of referrals to the program in a typical six-month period (December 15, 1966, to June 15, 1966) are as follows: [1]

Self (walk-in)	21 percent
Friend or relative	46
Other MFY programs	7
Other agencies	12
No information	14

These data suggest that the reputation of the program among the friends and relatives of applicants is the most significant factor affecting recruitment.

Intake

Once a potential trainee has been recruited into the program, he must pass through the intake process. The intake receptionist is the first person who speaks to applicants coming into the youth job center. The central concern during this critical period is to locate the trainee in a work-training situation as rapidly as possible. Early in the program's history it became apparent that any delay in getting a prospective trainee into the program was quite likely to result in a dropout, for out-of-school, disadvantaged youth—hard to reach in the first place—are easily discouraged by elaborate, bureaucratic processing procedures. Everything in the reception area, from the manner in which the intake worker greets applicants to the brightness of the chairs and decorations, is meant to

[1] "Eight-month Report to the Office of Manpower Policy, Evaluation and Research," (mimeographed, New York, Mobilization For Youth, December 16, 1955, to August 15, 1966), p. V–6. The actual number of referrals was 918.

reduce the applicant's apprehension, as is the room itself, which is hung with blown-up photographs of the various work sites, showing MFY trainees at work.

In 1962, a prospective trainee gave his name to a clerk and was quickly ushered in to see an employment counselor who, in turn, was charged with getting the client into a program as quickly as possible. It soon became apparent that a more individualized evaluation process was necessary to service clients properly. Clients were in fact dropping out of the program. Preprogram processing was amended so that a trainee's case folder, upon completion of a brief intake process, was forwarded to a supervisor, who in turn assigned the case to the specific counselor he believed could best work with the client. If the counselor had an opening in his case load, a telegram was sent to the youngster requesting him to return; if not, the applicant's name was put on a waiting list. This method of bringing counselors and clients together proved ineffective. Without a definite appointment to return, clients often preferred to stay away from the agency or to look for jobs on their own.

In 1965, when the research experiment began, the preprogram process became quite elaborate.[2] Prospective trainees had to submit to interviews two or three hours long, psychological testing batteries, and in some cases a two-week vocational-evaluation process (for which they were paid training stipends). The risk that clients would be alienated by the lengthy preprogram process had to be evaluated against the desirability of doing adequate research.

The overall strategy adopted was to minimize the waiting period and the number of people an enrollee had to see before getting to his vocational counselor. Several processing steps were therefore merged in the intake counselor's role. In addition to preparing the many official forms required by law and completing a two- to three-hour research and service interview, the intake counselor interprets the program and its services to the client. He then assigns him to a vocational counselor and a training or placement or evaluation program as required by the research design. The division tried to vary the number of intake workers with the enrollment demand, so that clients could get to intake within a day or two of reception, or

---

[2] See the chapter on "Overview of Employment Opportunities" in this volume for a description of this experiment.

even on the same day. (A receptionist first met the client, asked a few simple questions, and then assigned him to an intake worker.)

Despite these initial attempts to process clients efficiently, there was still a high preprogram dropout rate—at times as high as 50 percent. Statistical analysis revealed the fact that a disproportionate number of the dropouts were young Puerto Ricans. The division policy required that clients who needed working papers were to be told by intake counselors to get them and then return to the agency for vocational assignment. A large number of these youngsters, particularly Puerto Rican clients, never returned with their papers. Further investigation revealed that non-English-speaking youngsters have unique problems in obtaining papers: They often lack proof of their birth date; there are few Spanish-speaking personnel at the working-papers clinic; and the youngsters are often unable to understand directions on how to reach the clinic. An escort service was developed and has been successful in expediting this process. Similar assistance is provided for processing social-security applications. Procedures also have been instituted for securing birth-date certification from Puerto Rico.

To learn how preprogram attrition might be further reduced, a field study of a year's preprogram dropouts—434 youngsters—was made. The results clarified a number of assumptions made by the staff.

To save time and money, the initial attempt to contact the dropout population was made through the Post Office. Letters were sent informing the dropouts of the agency's wish to interview them in the near future. About one third of these letters (141) were undeliverable and returned. An additional eighty-three youngsters had moved out of the area or were not living at home. In sixty-four cases, home visits failed to locate the youths. Some twenty-three others were not reached or were unwilling to cooperate. Only 113 —less than one third—were actually interviewed in the survey.[3]

Several factors contribute to this low rate of response. One is the relatively high mobility of minority groups (partictularly Puerto

[3] Unfortunately, these interviews were not analyzed in terms of where in program processing the client dropped out—i.e., before or after the intake interview. The results indicate the difficulty of following up on clients either personally or by mail after a period of time has elapsed.

Ricans) in this area; another is the fact that many out-of-area youngsters give false addresses in order to get into MFY; and a third factor is that many trainees live with friends or relatives but failed to indicate the name in care of which their mail might be delivered.

The 131 interviewees gave the following reasons for not returning to MFY:

Found job on own	27 percent
Too much waiting or red tape	20
Ineligible	11
Family responsibilities or marriage	9
Stipend too low	6
Pregnancy or illness	6
Felt MFY could not help or was not interested	5
Trouble with birth certificates or social security	3
Moved away	3
Other or don't know	10
Total	100

The predominant reasons for not coming back seem to have been that the trainees went out and found jobs on their own or were disenchanted with the agency's red tape. Many enrollees were subjected to forces which Mobilization could not influence, such as the family's moving frequently, the lure of better-paying but poor-advancement jobs, illness, etc.

It was also clear from the study that the trainees perceived the agency in ways which differed from what Mobilization wished to project. For example, many enrollees had the misconception that the agency simply offered jobs.

The most encouraging finding of the survey was that 78 percent of the enrollees said that they would return to MFY if they ever needed employment help. Pursuing this clue, a follow-up unit was established. All broken appointments were followed up by an immediate home visit to encourage the enrollee to return or to find out why he would not. Preprogram loss was cut by 63 percent after this procedure was instituted.

Testing

Psychological and educational testing has generally not been regarded as a useful employment-evaluation or prediction tool at Mobilization. Test results are often inaccurate because of cultural biases in the tests or enrollees' emotional responses to the test-taking situation. Employment counselors have felt that they could make a reasonably accurate judgment of an enrollee's IQ, reading ability, and psychological state in the course of an extensive initial interview.

Nevertheless, with the launching of the controlled research experiment in 1965, research needs for educational testing of all clients were given priority.[4] The problem was to find an appropriate place within the program-processing sequence which would not interfere with rapid counselor-client engagement and the client's subsequent introduction into work training.

At first, testing was postponed until the trainee actually enrolled in a program. This ensured that counseling would be available to trainees who might balk at testing and, as an added incentive, that trainees would be paid during testing. Although this system made testing as attractive as possible, it was still not successful. Often, in order to capitalize on the availability of suitable training positions, counselors made referrals and placements outside of MFY immediately, without waiting for the clients to be tested. Once in training or on the job, trainees were less likely to attach significance to a non-work-related activity and often were reluctant to return for testing. Accordingly the preprogram sequence was altered so that all clients would be tested before entering work-training.

Currently, the system operates so as to ensure that about 90 percent of all active trainees are tested before entering a program and before scheduled job referrals. On the day after completing intake, the trainee meets with his assigned counselor for a half hour in the morning. After lunch at the MFY luncheonette, he returns to the agency for an afternoon of testing. The testing battery provides baseline data on trainees' reading and arithmetic ability,

[4] This testing was for purposes of evaluating the relative effectiveness of parts of the program and not necessarily for screening trainees for particular training sites. The scores nevertheless were available to counselors.

through the Gates Reading Test and the Wide Range Achievement Test in arithmetic. These two tests are administered to trainees again after a period in the program, and the differential scores are used to indicate the effectiveness of the remedial-education program.[5]

Along with this standard battery of tests, the testing service may administer a whole range of special tests of a psychological and vocational nature if a counselor so requests. These special tests include the WAIS Intelligence Test, the Thematic Apperception Test, the Bender Test, the Kuder Interest Test, and a number of more involved aptitude surveys. The administration of these special tests is time-consuming since they are given individually. Some counselors use these tests often and others only rarely, perhaps because they lack the ability to interpret the results. This possibility would suggest the advisability of in-service training for counselors who are unfamiliar with test interpretation.

Vocational Evaluation

Employment counselors frequently ask for help in evaluating the skill level, work habits, motivation, and attitudes of enrollees. The Vocational Evaluation Unit established in 1965 uses a work-sample technique to elicit this information. A work sample is a series of tasks which cover a range of activities common to a particular occupation. By observing an enrollee in the performance of these tasks the counselor can assess his mechanical aptitude, his affinity for the given occupation, and his ability to manage a work situation. Work samples have been developed for diverse occupational areas and can test different levels of skill development. For example, to demonstrate potential as an artisan jeweler, a trainee must display skill in the use of a jeweler's saw, needle files, pliers,

---

[5] All trainees receive the Revised Beta Intelligence Test. Boys get the Bennett Mechanical Comprehension Test and girls receive the Minnesota Clerical Test. The IPAT, a personality inventory, is also given to those trainees who have the ability to read it. These tests are also administered to trainees who speak only Spanish, the instructions of course being read in Spanish. A Spanish-language version of the Bennett Mechanical Test is also used. The Gates Reading Test is not given to those who cannot read English —approximately 31 percent of the trainee population.

and soldering and polishing equipment. He must also demonstrate a high degree of visual-motor coordination.

A good work-sample series, in addition to specifying the skills required for a given occupation, delineates such relevant information as the mental and physical characteristics required of workers, the typical work environment encountered, the tools and equipment usually used, and a suggestion of which jobs in other occupations are related in terms of these factors.

The key to the success of the evaluation is the evaluator himself, his ability to involve the client in the work-sample activities and his sensitivity to diagnostic clues in the client's performance. The evaluator needs to know when and for how long to provide warm-up activities prior to the performance upon which judgments are to be based, when to take a client off a task, when to try a task again, and, finally, how to interpret the client's performance in accordance with the industrial standards upon which the work sample is based. In addition to rating the client's work-relevant behavior, he is required to appraise the overall appearance of the end product, the degree of precision with which it was made, and the time it took to complete the task.

As originally designed, the Vocational Evaluation Unit accepted referrals of trainees in all phases of program: new enrollees without specific interests or known talents; trainees who had been unsuccessful at the types of training they wanted; youngsters ready for on-the-job training or direct placement who needed an accurate assessment of their skills, etc. A trainee remained in the unit as long as was necessary to obtain the proper evaluation. (A complete evaluation usually takes two weeks.) Employment counselors reported that the unit was a great help, and in over 90 percent of the cases they followed the recommendations of the unit.

However, a depth evaluation of the utility of the unit was lacking. The question was raised by the division director as to whether its evaluations were accurate enough to warrant its high cost. As part of the controlled research experiment, one aspect of the Vocational Evaluation Unit—its ability to assess new enrollees—was selected for closer examination. This area was chosen because it was the easiest to control in a systematic way.

After intake and before seeing an employment counselor, about half of the new enrollees are randomly assigned to the Evaluation Unit for two weeks. On the basis of the evaluation, an assignment to a counselor and a specific training program or direct placement is made. The object of the research is to determine if the unit can predict work success better than standard vocational counseling.

The results of the research experiment are not yet available, but even if they are negative, the unit may still be a useful program tool. Is the specific area in which the unit is being evaluated—its assessment of new enrollees—the most important of its possible functions? Past experience would suggest not. Most referrals to the unit had already been trainees in programs. On the other hand, perhaps the greatest value of the two-week stay in the unit will not be the evaluation proper, but the orientation aspect of the unit and its informality, lack of pressure, one-to-one relationship between evaluator and client. It is hoped that the research report will help to clarify this.

Conclusion

The preprogram processing and evaluation of enrollees are complex. Much thought and effort have gone into developing procedures which can fulfill data-collection tasks while sustaining an intelligent, concerned relationship with clients. From the service point of view, not considering the needs of specific research projects, experience recommends the following basic preprogramming processing and evaluation components: (1) an initial reception step to determine the applicant's eligibility; (2) an intake interview as soon after reception as possible, to collect descriptive employment information and to make an initial vocational assessment and training assignment; [6] (3) immediate assignment to a vocational

[6] In the opinion of some MFY staff, intake counselors do not necessarily have to be professionals. Intelligent indigenous adults can be trained to evaluate the employment experience, level of motivation, and general social level of deprived youths. Since the range of initial choices is limited in a typical youth-employment program, an intake counselor needs to know very little about training and employment per se. He must decide whether the enrollee should go to a vocational counselor specializing in direct placement and on-the-job training, to a vocational counselor in charge of a particular crew, or to a prevocational program for non-English-speaking trainees.

counselor who becomes the client's primary contact at the agency and is responsible for all referrals and specific vocational planning; (4) a small testing and vocational-evaluation unit, offering, on a referral basis, psychological and aptitude testing and/or assessment of mechanical aptitudes and work readiness in particular fields.

Although this paper has stressed the efforts made to ensure that clients receive the best service possible, a constant concern at Mobilization has been the problem of "displacement of goals" because of the requirements of various funding sources and administrative procedures. Suddenly fifty job slots open up and must be filled in two weeks. To meet the demands of the research design, 5 percent of the applicants must be assigned to non-MFY training sites. Because the program has a long waiting list of applicants, systematic efforts are not made to ensure that those most in need of training are in fact coming to the agency.

Any large employment program offering a variety of services that involve detailed processing procedures will develop a tendency to operate so as to satisfy its own needs for efficiency, the requirements of funding sources, and the personal needs of its administrators and staff as opposed to the needs of its clients. Probably the only way to counter such tendencies is to have them constantly brought to the attention of administrators of programs. At MFY, operations or feedback research staff attempted to do this through systematic compilation of program statistics, follow-up on selected segments of the trainee population, and periodic appraisals of particular training components.

3

Work Crews and Dispersed Work

Burton Weinstein

The majority of work-program trainees at MFY were assigned either to one of MFY's work crews or to one of its dispersed-work sites. The Mobilization work crews provide a sheltered work environment on Mobilization premises, where trainees work in small groups under the direct supervision of crew chiefs. Supervision is immediate and intensive, and the work pace can be easily controlled. Dispersed-work sites, on the other hand, offer training and work experience outside the agency. Trainees are placed in hospitals, the fire and police departments, the housing authority, the department of parks, and other like agencies. The tone of the dispersed work site is considerably different from that of a crew. Individual trainees are placed in an already existing work place, and they work alongside the regular adult staff. Supervision is provided by the normal supervisory personnel at the work site. These supervisors are not chosen for their ability to deal with the trainees' problems or for their teaching abilities.

There has been considerable disagreement over the years over the respective merit of these systems. One of the major questions to be answered in the research study goes to this issue.[1]

Another program and policy dispute has revolved around whether training at these sites should emphasize specific job skills or work habits and attitudes, training for specific jobs in which labor shortages exist or for general improvement in employability.

[1] See the discussion of the research project in the chapter on "Overview of Employment Opportunities" in this volume.

Experience over the years in the crews and dispersed sites considerably clarifies this latter issue as well as the relative merits of dispersed and crew sites.

The Work Crews

MFY's Work Training Program currently administers twelve work crews operating in nine occupational areas. The total trainee capacity of the crews is almost three hundred. The crews differ from one another in the emphasis on the development of occupational skills. It must be noted that Mobilization's mandate is from the Neighborhood Youth Corps, which provides for "a steady progression of work experience" with only "some vocational training." [2] Some of MFY's shops seem to follow this mandate while others are run with a stricter skill-training emphasis. It appears that the closer the link between training and the job market, the more likely emphasis will be put on job skills. Thus the luncheonette, building-repair crews, and woodshop, which have the poorest labor-market links—readily available jobs for graduates—tend to get youngsters who are the least able or ready for skill training. This occurs partly because these youngsters tend not to express a preference for a work area and partly because their counselors tend to view them as unable to meet the demands of the other crews.

[2] The Neighborhood Youth Corps was authorized under the Economic Opportunity Act of 1964. Operating under the aegis of the U.S. Department of Labor, the program consists of in-school, out-of-school, and summer programs. The in-school program provides part-time work and on-the-job training for high-school-age youths of low-income families. The summer program provides these youths with job opportunities during the summer months. The out-of-school program for sixteen-to-twenty-one-year-olds provides work experience and training, with the emphasis on helping youth acquire work habits that improve their employability. The original Neighborhood Youth Corps stipend was $1.25 per hour. Since February 1967, this has been raised to $1.50 an hour. The stipend for the in-school and summer programs has remained $1.25 an hour.

The Manpower Development and Training programs (MDTA), authorized under legislation passed in 1962, 1964, and 1966, emphasized occupational training rather than work experience for the unemployed and the underemployed who cannot obtain full-time employment without training. It also provides basic education where required. It allows for payment of allowances including transportation and subsistence for up to 104 weeks to eligible persons. The program is for both youths and adults.

The higher level crews—hospital, auto repair, jewelry, and clerical
—focus more heavily on the development of occupational skills.
These shops have much closer ties to the labor market, since there
is a shortage of workers in these areas.

The *jewelry shop* is designed primarily to teach the specific and
general work skills necessary for basic entry-level jobs in the mass-
production jewelry industry. Work-adjustment elements do not receive major emphasis. The jewelry industry in New York City is in
need of workers, and successful graduates of this shop are almost
assured of a successful placement. Thus the training element in this
shop is stressed.

MFY's *clerical shop* consists of a double program. A clerical-
training shop offers instruction in typing, setting up letters and
documents, cutting stencils, mimeo, IBM key punch, arithmetic,
spelling, and English. A second component in the clerical area consists of students in clerical jobs outside of the shop. These students
must follow the work rules and procedures of their work places.
In effect, they are short-term clerical workers who receive the regular Neighborhood Youth Corps stipend. Trainees in MFY's clerical
shop generally have completed at least some high school, and
many attend night school.

When the clerical shop was first established, it sought to train its
youngsters by having them do clerical jobs for the agency and work
solicited from outside sources as well. The shop's experience was
that the quality of the work produced was not at a satisfactory
level. In a subsequent reorganization, the notion of doing "real
work" was discarded, and the shop took on more of the aspects of a
classroom than a work place. This reorientation toward a structured, teaching-based program has proved more successful in raising the level of the trainees' clerical skills. The clerical shop has a
direct labor-market link, and its placement record has been very
good.

Mobilization's *hospital program* is run at two hospitals in the
area which offer a variety of training positions—x-ray technician,
file clerk, dental assistant, receptionist, clinic aide, food-service
aide, nurse's aide, and lab technician. These training positions are
designed primarily for girls who are at a high educational level.
Though the crew chiefs are MFY employees, the control that the

agency can exert over these training positions is limited by the demands of the hospitals. This program is designed to fill the hospital's labor requirements, and it has been very successful; over 30 percent of the trainees have been hired by the hospital in which they were trained, while many other trainees have found employment in the medical-services area elsewhere.

Mobilization's *sewing shop* is open to both boys and girls and is one of the few training areas that can successfully place non-English-speaking girls. The orientation of the shop is toward job placement. Power-sewing-machine operators are in great demand in New York City. The shop operates with no outside production demands except that the trainees are required to produce the equivalent of industry piecework norms. Trainees are not deemed ready for placement until they have acquired the skills to meet these work norms. The sewing shop has had an excellent record of placement, even though there are no prescreening of trainees and no entrance requirements.

The *furniture-finishing shop* teaches the major areas of furniture refinishing: repair of nicks, burns, and scratches, finish removal, spraying, french polishing, color matching, and polishing. This shop, like the jewelry shop, was initiated because of labor-market shortages, and graduates are almost assured of jobs. As a result the shop's emphasis is on the acquisition of the necessary job-connected skills. There are no production demands except those that the crew chief can devise for training purposes. Although it is a relatively new training site, it has been quite successful in placing trainees on jobs.

The *woodworking/cabinet shop* is open to both English- and non-English-speaking boys. Many of the industrial skills taught are transferable to other machine-operator jobs. Trainees learn to use the standard machines found in commercial woodworking firms, and the use of these machines for production work is stressed. The shop has built kitchen cabinets, chess tables, chairs, sofas, bookcases, and many specialty items. There is no production demand per se, but the facilities of the shop have often been used to build items for the agency.

The woodworking industry in New York City consists largely of many small specialty manufacturers, and the area has not been sufficiently studied by MFY's job developers. It is possible that there may be a labor-market link from this shop.

The purpose of MFY's *luncheonette* is to provide work-adjustment training. To a lesser extent, it also serves to teach the skills necessary for eventual employment in the food-trades industry. The luncheonette operates as a business serving both Mobilization employees and trainees and the general public. The work flow of the luncheonette has been broken down into the following areas: table service, fountain service, take-out service, cashier, kitchen, grill. This breakdown is intended to provide a graded introduction to the work. Under ideal conditions, a trainee will start out in the area of least pressure and gradually work into the more demanding areas—waitress, counterman, short-order cook, etc.

Staff includes a manager, an assistant manager, and a cook. Since the luncheonette operates as a business, it is subject to skewed production pressures. Although a three-man staff is adequate for supervision and training during part of the working day, it cannot combine training and supervision with meeting the demands of customers during the peak business hours. At certain times of the day the physical plant can be run almost as a sheltered workshop while at the peak times the work pace and its production demands are frantic.

Mobilization's luncheonette, like its Shell station, served to demonstrate that, when work training is carried out in an environment that is subject to unmanaged production pressures, the demands of the training site must usually give way to those of production.

The MFY *building-repair crews* were set up when the training program opened in 1962. During the five years of their operation they have performed much useful work for Mobilization itself as well as for other public agencies in the area. The link between these crews and the labor market has been, at best, a very tenuous one— the construction industry in the area goes through periodic doldrums, and the unions involved have a history of bias.

Building-repair crews have always had to operate under production pressures that could not be managed by their crew chiefs, much of the training that takes place tends to be regulated by these pressures rather than trainee needs. In the past, these crews were used as holding tanks—trainees who did not fit into any of the agency's other crews were assigned to building repair. As more and more of the least able trainees were assigned to these crews, the quality of training was forced down also, and on the next round, the circle repeated itself. Mobilization has tried to correct this problem by eliminating several of these crews and assigning better-qualified trainees to them.[3] A totally unstructured program is gradually giving way to a rudimentary but sequential training program.

Training in auto mechanics at MFY's *auto shop* would seem to lend itself to a structured and sequential program. There is little, if any, need to use "live" automobiles in most phases of this training. Moreover, the use of real automobiles can complicate the trainees' problems. If the car belongs to a customer, the training element in its repair will be slight: The trainee cannot make mistakes and cannot learn from them; the crew chief must give too much of his attention to those working on the car so as to prevent error; finally, there is the pressure to finish the job and return the car to its owner.

Yet, MFY's auto-repair shop began as a real garage which took in cars from the public, repaired them, and returned them to their owners. The pressures of production and the program structure that evolved resulted in a haphazard method of training. There was, in short, production without program. Though efforts have been made to restructure the auto shop toward teaching, these have not been entirely successful. In other words, this shop has suffered from its early commitment to a relatively unprotected form of training which laid emphasis on production.

The danger of such an emphasis is even more graphically shown in the history of the MFY *Shell station*. One of the first training sites established by MFY was a service station leased from the Shell Oil Company. The physical plant was average for this type of station—three repair bays and two pump islands. The station was designed to service the public and was therefore subject to the

---

[3] The reluctance to assign such trainees is based on the difficulty of placing them on the job after the completion of training. Bias in unions and apprenticeship programs is at the root of the problem.

production demands of any private gasoline service station. Because it served the public, the production demands at the station were not easily controlled. The station, unlike most others, did not engage in mechanical repair work to any marked degree; its primary services consisted of pumping gas and the general lubrication of cars along with tire repair, sales, etc.

As a training area, the Shell station could not pay off. The industry generally is faced with a labor shortage—but not for attendants. The average staff of a gasoline station is about three, and the volume of gas that such a station can sell in a business day does not warrant the hiring of a full-time pump jockey, with exceptions perhaps at peak periods. Generally the attendant's work is done on a catch-as-catch-can basis by the station's mechanic or his helper. Counselors' problems were compounded further because the nature of the job is such that only English-speaking trainees were eligible for training at the station. Furthermore, one of the requirements for employment in auto service is a driver's license, for which the eligibility age is eighteen. Most of MFY's trainee population is now younger than that.

Work Crew Log Program

As we have noted, a major question that has confronted the crew program is whether it should concentrate on job training or on work adjustment. Because the trainees vary considerably in their work and skill capabilities, it was decided that the program would provide both work-training and job adjustment in varying combinations in the different shops. In areas with close links to the job market, the crews tend to provide mostly job training. Crews such as building repair, which do a more general kind of work orientation and in which there is very little related job placement following completion, tend to emphasize work adjustment.

Experience suggests that work adjustment cannot be taught when a real job is not waiting at the end of training. The best motivation for successful work adjustment is the desire for a specific job. The crews with clear links to the labor market made a far superior record to the unlinked crews.

It is also true that the more able trainees were generally steered into the job-linked crews; yet the fact that poor work habits were the major reason for firing trainees placed in jobs [4] indicates that the nonlinked crews were not successful in their work-orientation and adjustment training. Some have contended that, given the nature of the trainee population, it is likely that many trainees would have work-adjustment problems even if training were provided only in areas where good labor-market links exist. As one observer noted, "You can't teach a skill in a crew if trainees don't attend regularly." Although this contention is probably correct, it is also likely that adjustment problems are more easily dealt with in the context of "a job at the end of training."

For example, since trainees have varying abilities and enter crews at different points in time, training can get quite confused if sufficient staff isn't available for individual attention. The crews with labor-market links tended to develop sequential progressions of skill levels for trainees to pass through, since the crew chief had to be able to certify a trainee as ready for placement on a real job. Nonlabor-market-linked crews tended not to develop systematic instruction and thus lacked the structure around which to inculcate work adjustment. Absences mean less when it is not clear what will be missed or what will be lost by being absent.

The fact of training in a particular field, however, even with good related placement prospects, is no guarantee that a trainee is prepared adequately for the future. Adolescents are learning about their environment constantly, trying different activities, experimenting, confirming interests and changing them; it is unrealistic to expect a sixteen- or seventeen-year-old to make a vocational commitment for life, and it is particularly unrealistic to expect this commitment from a disadvantaged youth, whose vocational horizons are limited and whose self-image, in many cases, is conditioned negatively by parents and friends who are underemployed or unemployed.

To supplement the trainee's limited knowledge of occupational opportunities and their requirements, a new program was initiated in October 1966. For each crew a series of special activities was developed and coordinated with the basic skill training being pro-

---

[4] See the chapter on "The Problem of Job Placement" in this volume for a discussion of this issue.

vided. The purpose of these special activities was to give the trainee an opportunity to see what other occupations are like and to decide if he had an interest in exploring other occupational possibilities.

This activity is also important because it helps to resolve an operational dilemma. On the basis of experience, Mobilization practiced rapid placement into training, rather than prolonged pre-training testing and counseling.[5] This meant that a trainee might be placed without a real opportunity to explore his abilities and interests. The risk is that the youngster may inadvertently be pigeonholed. The special activities encourage the trainee's exploration of additional training possibilities even though he is learning a skill. They reinforce the agency's commitment to the idea that a trainee may change his mind at any stage of training.

The special activities, or Log Program, were planned on a six-month basis to conform to the length of time the trainee ideally spends in a crew-training program. Each month has a main theme: occupations and training related to particular areas; unrelated occupations and training; preparation for placement; community agencies which offer employment services; other social services, etc.

The Log Program also sought to encourage the identification of the trainee with the agency. For example, the trainee should know that he may return to the agency at any time—whether he is employed or unemployed, in need, or for a social visit—and that there are other services available should they be needed: legal services, family services, child care, education, etc.

For each of the monthly themes, three to five activities were planned, including field trips, and the trainees were given an opportunity to perform a different trade activity in the shop. The specific content of each activity is determined by the crew chief, the counselor, the supervisor, and occasionally by the trainees themselves.

Although most staff agreed that the Log Program served a useful purpose, some contended that it was an essentially rational approach to the problem of lack of motivation and clear vocational goals, and that these problems must also be addressed at the emotional level. These staff members have urged that the informal relationships that develop among trainees be tapped to support the

[5] See the chapter on "The Processing of the Trainee" in this volume for an analysis of the reasons behind this procedure.

vocational goals of training. They suggest the development of a variety of social and recreational activities—dances, athletic teams, etc.—and also the formation of a trainee union which might sponsor not only such activitites but also social-action campaigns against bias in the building trades and the like.

Crew Chiefs

The key element in the crew program is the crew chief. He is the foreman of the crew, and it is his responsibility not only to teach the skills and requisite attitudes but also to serve as a role model for the trainees. He must be someone with whom they can identify, someone whom they can emulate.

Mobilization has always sought to hire crew chiefs who were both master craftsmen and master teachers, but this has seldom been possible. In addition, the types of crew chiefs hired at different times reflected the policy concerns of the agency. Initially, in 1962 and 1963, the emphasis was on trainees doing real work; the crews were to be as close as possible to real work sites and situations. There was a total identification with the rough, tough world of working men, and the crew chiefs brought to Mobilization reflected this. In the old days the counselor was hardly allowed on the work site, and crew chiefs were able to make unilateral decisions that could not easily be contested. Today a crew chief must coexist with the counselor and must also function under a type of supervision which is geared more to understanding developmental needs of trainees.[6] One area in which the agency has been particularly remiss is in in-service training for crew chiefs. Such training would probably have gone a great way toward alleviating some of the strains between counselor and crew chief and problems engendered by the emphasis on work adjustment in some of the crews.

A crew chief is, of course, the staff person most intimately involved with the trainee. He succeeds to the extent that he is able to motivate the trainee toward work, and fails when he is unable to achieve this. This is a difficult task, especially since a large per-

---

[6] Since 1966 counselors for a particular crew and the crew chief have been responsible to a single supervisor who conducts weekly case conferences where individual trainee problems are reviewed.

centage of the trainees initially exhibit apathy and defeatism. Although crew chiefs have the authority to dock a trainee's pay and suspend him, if a trainee ultimately leaves the program as a result, nothing is gained. Likewise, nothing is gained if he remains but continually absents himself and disregards training rules.

The agency was fortunate in having a number of crew chiefs who showed great concern for the trainees: "I hate to suspend a kid, and they all know it . . . so I rarely have to do it." Of course, not all crew chiefs have been so sensitive, and those who have not often develop conflicts with the counselors. The agency's best crew chiefs are able to identify with the trainees but also possess the ability to step out of the trainees' arena when necessary.

While all crew chiefs had been employed in their particular trades for many years before coming to Mobilization, few of them had ever taught their trades. Some of the chiefs proved to be natural-born teachers; others were able to develop their teaching skills, without the press of discipline and other motivational problems. The agency was fortunate in having some match between available crew chiefs and the requisites needed for chiefs in various crews.

The greatest value of the crews to Mobilization's work-training program—their accessibility—is also one of their greatest sources of difficulty and problems. The same crew is often used for a variety of purposes. For a trainee with severe emotional problems, it is seen as a sheltered workshop. The same crew at the same time may be used for another trainee whose motivation is quite good and who needs to learn skills. For a third, an intermediate type of trainee, the same crew may be a means of orientation in work adjustment and habits. These multiple goals put considerable strain on a crew chief.

Dispersed Work

Dispersed work consists of placing trainees in Federal, state, or city agencies, both public and private, where supervision is provided by the regular agency supervisory staff. Approximately three hundred such placements were regularly available at Mobilization. Dispersed work differs from crew training in a number of significant areas: Individual trainees are placed alongside adult employees rather than in peer groups; a trainee's immediate supervisor is not specifically trained or chosen for his ability to teach or relate to the trainee; the degree of control that Mobilization can exercise over these dispersed work sites is severely limited in that most contact between the dispersed-work site and Mobilization may be filtered through another organization, such as the city agency which administers the funds for the program.

Examples of Dispersed-Work Sites and Training Areas

Site	*Area*
St. Luke's School	Nursery aide
Veterans' Administration Hospital	File clerk
	Dental assistant
	Laboratory technician aide
Commonwealth of Puerto Rico	Bookkeeper aide
	Library aide
	Stock clerk
General Services Administration	Clerk-typist
	Maintenance man
Legal Aid Society	Clerical aide
	File clerk
Veterans' Administration Hospital	Orderly
	Laboratory assistant
	Nurses' aide
Brooklyn Jewish Hospital	EKG assistant
	Nurses' aide
	Clerk-typist
New School for Social Research	Library aide
St. John's Episcopal Hospital	Medical records clerk
	Food-service aide

Unlike the communication problems generated by an in-house program such as the crews—which, although they may be difficult, are at least confined to one set of operators with a single set of ground rules—the dispersed program required contact with four separate organizations: the referral agency (MFY), the job site, the supervising agency, and finally, the Neighborhood Youth Corps itself.

Mobilization, acting here as the referral agent, provides the trainee with counseling, vocational evaluation, and remedial education. The dispersed job site furnishes the training and immediate supervisory personnel. The supervising agency—the New York City Department of Personnel or the New York Community Council—has the responsibility of providing field representatives who serve as liaison between the job site, the referring agency, and the Neighborhood Youth Corps. The Neighborhood Youth Corps has the responsibility for verifying the trainee's eligibility for the program, processing all relevant forms, and issuing the trainee a check for his training time.

The operation of this dispersed-work program has given rise to a number of difficulties, many of which were caused by or complicated by the structure of the dispersed program itself. The agencies which furnish Mobilization's dispersed-work slots have very few Spanish-speaking supervisors and, except for low-level maintenance jobs—which trainees are reluctant to accept and counselors to offer—very few jobs have been made available for trainees whose English is severely limited. For those trainees who attend Mobilization's remedial-education classes, this problem is even more acute, for the job-site supervisors are reluctant to employ a trainee on a half-time basis. This is to be expected because the production demands at the work site are not manageable and do not change because one of the workers happens to be a Mobilization trainee.

Along with a lack of suitable jobs, the subcontractual nature of dispersed work has resulted in other problems. Trainees have had their dispersed jobs disappear from under them—departments have been reorganized and a "dispersed slot" eliminated without communication back to the referral agency. Some of these work slots have been filled by job-site supervisors who promoted other workers rather than fill the job with a trainee.

To prevent disruption of the work on the job sites, the Neighborhood Youth Corps' policy does not permit the staff of Mobilization or any other referring agency to visit the job sites. Further-more, they are not allowed to deal directly with the job-site supervisor; all communication regarding a trainee must be channeled through the Neighborhood Youth Corps field representative. Forcing a trainee's crew chief and counselor to communicate through an intermediary would be absolute folly in a crew situation. In dispersed work it makes even less sense, because the trainee is, for most purposes, out of touch with his counselor, and the job-site supervisor is the only communication link between trainee and counselor. In most cases a counselor whose client was at a dispersed job was not contacted unless a problem came up—and even then there were delays.

Many of the jobs that have been offered to Mobilization have differed markedly from their description. Trainees have been sent to these jobs, have not been hired, and have subsequently dropped out of the training program. The N.Y.C. Department of Personnel issues very general job descriptions, which may serve the purpose for which they were designed but are of little value to the dispersed-work referral agency. A clerical aide in the Department of Hospitals may be a quite different job from a clerical aide in the sheriff's office, and both jobs may be significantly different from a clerical aide in the Housing Authority.

In response to these problems, restrictions on direct communication with the job sites were eased in 1966. The administrative mechanism of the Neighborhood Youth Corps has been reorganized, and in many areas communication between the participants has significantly improved. On those job sites formerly administered by the Community Council, the referring agency has assumed the supervision of its trainees at the job sites. The referral agency (MFY), now able to deal directly with the job-site supervisor, has been able to determine the precise job requirements of the training slot, and most of the misuses that were characteristic of the old structure have been eliminated. Better contact between referral agent and work site has also resulted in the development of jobs that are a closer match for the trainee's abilities and has enabled Mobilization to begin placing its Spanish-speaking trainees in other than low-level menial jobs.

The reorganization and the consequent elimination of the outside field representative have served to narrow the differences between some of Mobilization's crews and the dispersed-work sites. The hospital crew and the student clerical unit are essentially dispersed training vehicles; trainees work along with adults, are supervised by personnel at the work place, and perform the normal work of their assigned work site. In effect, the sole difference between these crews and a regular dispersed job was in the nature of the supervision—the presence of the outside field representative in dispersed-work situations. With this supervisory role taken over by Mobilization's staff, the dispersed trainee also has what amounts to a dual counselor, his regular MFY counselor as well as Mobilization's field representative. This extra dose of communication between the cooperating staff of a single agency has proved to be a marked benefit to the individual dispersed trainee, in that problems in communication between trainee and counselor are easier to work out if there is an interested third party involved.

Work Crew and Dispersed Work—Comparative Value

Dispersed work offers an array of possible training positions that are far beyond the capabilities of even the most ambitious crew-training program. This is especially true when training entails the use of large pieces of capital equipment and specialized technical personnel.

Dispersed-work sites are not purchased or rented. The referring agency does not staff or maintain them in any way. They are, in effect, cost-free training sites. There are costs involved, of course, but their impact is not on the referring agency. This allows the training agency to exercise considerable freedom of movement. It can pick up new training sites, and it can drop others. Such freedom is totally impossible with an in-house crew program. Mobilization has certainly added new crews, changed the face of others, and even dropped several, but this is always a very slow and costly process.

Dispersed work, for all its good points, is not a faultless training vehicle. Many job sites are reluctant to accept trainees for half-time work because it may upset their work schedules to do so. It is difficult to locate acceptable jobs for Spanish-speaking trainees, and some types of job cannot be found in those agencies which offer dispersed job slots. It is, for instance, virtually impossible for Mobilization to locate a power-sewing-machine operator's job for a dispersed client. The check that a counselor can have on his client's progress in an MFY crew may be complete and immediate, more so than is ever possible with dispersed work. There is, additionally, the risk that a trainee's job will be abused; in the past, trainees on dispersed jobs have been pigeonholed into low-level jobs at their work places. Trainees have run mimeograph machines for two weeks straight because the work-site supervisor had a deadline to meet, and other trainees have washed engines instead of learning to repair them.

Of the two training strategies, the work crew is the more expensive program. It may be that crew training is better suited to youngsters with emotional problems and deficits in education, who may require a relatively slow and controlled pace in a protective and supportive environment. On the other hand, the insulation that crew training provides may make it more difficult for a trainee to operate successfully in a regular job after he leaves the crew. But dispersed work, while providing the trainee with a real work environment, may prove too difficult for a youth with very limited skills and education.

With the exception of clerical training, crew work tends to be concentrated mainly in the vocational blue-collar areas: sewing, construction, automotives, food trades, hospital services. Dispersed work includes many of the crew areas but also opens up a myriad of training possibilities in areas that are impossible for an agency to duplicate.

The two training strategies also differ in the quantity and possibly the quality of the counseling that can take place. Crew training offers a useful vehicle for effective counseling in that a great deal of feedback is possible between the counselor and the crew chief. The trainee is also more available for counseling and can, if necessary, be released from his training site for counseling sessions. The crew setup also provides a good vehicle for group counseling, a technique which, for many trainees at dispersed sites, is a physical and administrative impossibility. Besides being separated physically, trainees cannot easily be released from their jobs because of the need to maintain the normal production-oriented pace of work.

Both the crew and the dispersed strategy have their merits, as indicated, and it is not clear whether the benefits of one are so great as to warrant scrapping the other. It may be concluded from the MFY experience that both are needed in programs that serve the broad spectrum of low-income youth.[7]

---

[7] A major goal of the research project is to more clearly specify the relative merits of both.

4

Advanced and Posttraining Programs: On-the-Job Training, and Direct Placement

Burton Weinstein

MFY's Job Development Unit is responsible for providing job opportunities for clients who complete work-training programs and are ready for upgrading as well as for clients who already have enough skills to obtain and hold a job. In addition to a director, there are six staff members, who deal directly with employers and union officials in the areas for which clients are trained or otherwise qualified; develop on-the-job-training situations, and follow up clients and employers after such training placements have been made; and follow up job leads obtained from the mass media or as a result of MFY publicity. Information about the requirements and qualifications of clients comes from job-order solicitation forms, which are filled out by counselors. These include a short profile of the client with suggested areas of placement or training.

The youth, lack of facility in English, and marginal ability of trainees have always been problems in finding jobs for them. There has also been a problem of having jobs available at the time when trainees are ready for them. Jobs on a relatively unskilled level are in great demand. When they do come available, they often disappear before trainees can be told of them. To cope with these problems, the unit has sought to establish contact with firms that have a steady need for less skilled help: food-service chains, hospitals, hotels, and the like.

Many methods are employed in attempting to locate jobs: public-education campaigns; personal contact wth individual employers and groups of employers; mail and telephone solicitation of employers; the formation of an advisory council made up of union and industry representatives to help develop ongoing contacts with business organizations and trade unions.[1]

The basic job-development technique involves telephone solicitation and visits to employers. Telephone solicitation is a relatively superficial job-search method intended to place a trainee on a job as fast as possible. MFY's past contacts, the classified phone directory, and newspaper want ads are culled to see if openings are available in particular work areas—and the process continues until a willing employer is located. Unfortunately, experience has shown that, even when an employer is found, there may be error caused by incomplete or inaccurate information. In brief telephone conversations the specifications of a job are often given imprecisely. The employer found in this manner has only a superficial knowledge of what the trainee will be like, and the trainee himself generally knows very little about the place he is being sent to. Because of these considerable shortcomings, telephone solicitation is used only to locate a stopgap job, until something better can be found. Jobs so solicited are generally in the area of general factory help, messengers, and the like.

Field workers account for most of the jobs developed for trainees. Paralleling the crew structure, the field workers are assigned to employment areas which can serve as outlets for crew training. When a new employer contact is made, a member of the job-development staff calls the prospective employer and arranges for an interview. At the interview the job developer finds out the exact nature of the job the trainee will perform and has a chance to check on the working conditions. The employer is advised of the nature of Mobilization's program and is made aware that he will not be sent a "finished" worker. At times employers balk at hiring such youngsters, but in the long run it is better to risk the loss of a placement than to risk alienating both an employer and a shakily motivated youngster.

[1] For a discussion of the unit's attempts to persuade employers to redefine job qualifications as well as to create news jobs, see the chapter on "The Problem of Job Placement" in this volume.

The most useful part of the field worker's job, apart from exchanging information with employers, is his attempt to bend the employers' hiring requirements to fit the trainees' skills. Field workers have also at times been able to convince an employer to waive a preemployment screening test or disregard its results.[2] In addition, if, after a placement is made, an employer is dissatisfied with a trainee's performance, job-development staff can often prevent a hasty firing at least for long enough to investigate if not solve the problem.

Job development is quite time-consuming and often frustrating. Discussions with employers do not always turn up jobs. Field workers average ten to fifteen employer contacts per week. Many more hours are spent in emergency calls and visits to employers in an attempt to deal with friction between trainees and fellow employees or employers. There are two basic approaches to job development: One can start with a trainee and attempt to develop a job for him, or find a job first and then look for an appropriate trainee. Of these approaches, the first takes longer, but generally results in better placement—the more that is known about the trainee, the more suitable his placement will be. In view of the comparatively small size of the staff, they have been hard pressed to follow this method consistently.

On-the-Job Training

On-the-job-training placements are made in firms, large and small, in a variety of occupational areas. Since 1964, approximately 175 trainees per year have been placed in on-the-job training, individually or in groups. Trainees are given eight to twenty weeks of specialized training in actual work settings while being paid at the standard labor-market entry rate for that job. Participating employers receive up to $25 a week per trainee as reimbursement for the training services provided.

Prior to placement, each on-the-job-training situation is investigated to determine whether it will enhance trainees' chances for future employment and whether the occupational field has the po-

---

[2] See the chapter on "The Problem of Job Placement" in this volume for a full discussion of this point.

tential for stable employment and opportunities for advancement. When an on-the-job-training situation is recommended by the MFY field counselor, it is reviewed by the director of Job Development and then submitted to the U. S. Bureau of Apprenticeship and Training for final approval. In this process, the Bureau of Apprenticeship and Training personnel are helpful in identifying occupations in which formal apprenticeship training can be initiated upon completion of the on-the-job training.[3]

Before a youth is placed in on-the-job training, his vocational counselor reviews his skills, abilities, interests, and work experience. The trainee must have exhibited sufficient maturity to meet the demands of a job, as well as the ability to learn a new or more advanced skill. Once he is on the job, the MFY field representative checks his progress by calling or visiting the employer. Counseling is also available after placement, but it is often difficult to arrange.

Some of the strengths of the on-the-job-training program are indicated in Herman and Sadofsky's appraisal:

> It offers the employer a number of inducements, including partial defrayal of the costs of training a new worker and a training program specifically suited to his needs as well as those of the trainee. In addition, the work program shares with the employer the risk of taking in an inexperienced employee by partially subsidizing him. In turn, the employer agrees to train the youth and often hires him as a permanent employee, though this is not necessarily part of the OJT agreement. For the youth, training occurs in an actual rather than a simulated work setting, and a one-to-one instructional relationship with an experienced worker or foreman is possible. Moreover, his compensation during the period of OJT far exceeds the training allowance which he receives as a pre-vocational or occupational trainee.[4]

As of July 1968, almost one thousand on-the-job-training contracts had been written by Mobilization, most of them in the cleri-

---

[3] Over the years very few trainees were placed in the apprenticeable trades, especially the building trades, largely because most unions in these trades have a history of bias.

[4] Melvin Herman and Stanley Sadofsky, *Youth-Work Programs* (New York, New York University Graduate School of Social Work, 1966), p. 144.

cal area. While potentially a valuable training strategy, many employers, especially the larger firms, have been reluctant to undertake the paper work of negotiating and following through on contract stipulations. In addition, the rate of successful completion of on-the-job training by trainees was only about 50 percent. Lack of skill and poor work habits, ordinary youthful immaturity, desire for other types of work, health problems, movement out of the city contributed to this result.[5]

Trade Training

MFY offers formal trade-school training to those whose vocational or academic skills warrant more advanced preparation. Youngsters may be selected for this training if they are able to meet certain criteria: The trainee must have a good idea of the demands of such training; he must have a realistic notion of what the trade can offer him; and he must have shown, while in Mobilization's crew- or dispersed-work program, that he has sufficiently developed his work habits and attitudes. The counselor selects an appropriate trade school with the trainee and in consultation with the Job Development Unit.

The staff of the Job Development Unit is responsible for maintaining up-to-date information on the many trade schools in the city, helping the counselor to make an appropriate choice, and meeting regularly with each trainee who attends a trade school. In addition to receiving periodic visits from the field representative, every full-time trainee is seen weekly by his counselor. The counselor thus has the opportunity to monitor the trainee's progress and problems. The schools are required to submit monthly reports on the trainee. If a trainee has excessive or unusual absences, for example, the trade school must report them immediately to the counselor.

Mobilization first entered the trade-school area through a demonstration grant provided by the Lavanburg-Corner House Foundation in February 1963. The prospective trainees were screened, so that those trainees selected for trade schools would be good

[5] An analysis of success and failure in the work programs is made in the chapter on "An Appraisal of Youth Employment Programs" in this volume.

training risks. They were, according to one report, "the cream of Mobilization's usual target group."

Trainees enrolled in the courses received a weekly stipend of $15 in addition to full tuition. In occasional cases of hardship engendered by double fares, etc., this stipend was increased to $20 weekly. Those trainees who were working while attending trade school were requested to pay fifty cents per hour of training, the average cost of tuition being seventy-five cents per hour. In the majority of cases the client population demonstrated good faith by paying this fee scrupulously.

Of the sixty-seven Lavanburg-sponsored youngsters, forty-eight took a total of fifty-one vocational courses, and four of this group also took driver-training courses. The remaining nineteen trainees were enrolled in driver-training courses only. The trade-training areas selected by the trainees are as follows:

Accounting and retail management	Machine repairs
Architectural drafting	Machine-shop practice
Barbering	Mechanical dentistry
Beauty culture	Mortuary science
Bookkeeping and typing	Practical nursing
Burroughs operator	Printing (multilith)
Data processing	Secretarial
Dental assistant	Sewing shop (pressing)
Dietetics	Stenography
Executive secretary	Technical drawing
Fashion designing	Television repair
Keypunch operator	Welding

The diversity of courses selected emphasizes one of the purposes of the Lavanburg-Mobilization project: to make available a greater selection of training opportunities than was to be found in the then-current Federal, state, or city programs.

So few trade-training programs are available because the Manpower Development and Training Act courses are required to be set up on the basis of significant current labor-market shortages. While we believe that job openings for trade-school graduates must be available, it is our contention that the Manpower Development and Training Act method does not provide a young person the opportunity to select from the many other trade programs available where job openings do exist, but in smaller numbers than in the occupational shortage areas listed. . . . What we are demonstrating moves quite close to the free choice of schools which was available under the G. I. Bill of Rights.[6]

The results of the Lavanburg-MFY experiment are interesting in view of the fact that they represent the experiences of selected trainees in areas which they chose for themselves. A relatively low rate of completion was associated with the younger (sixteen and seventeen years) trade-training youth. Of the trainees aged seventeen or younger, only 50 percent completed training; of those aged eighteen years and over, 85 percent completed. It appears that programs must expect proportionately less completion for this younger group in more difficult courses.

There appeared to be no significant difference in course-completion rate between high-school graduates and dropouts, and little or no relationship between school-grade completed and the completion of formal trade training. Since most of the dropouts had left school early (ninth or tenth grade), these findings in regard to their ability to complete trade training may be of great importance. It appears that high-school dropouts can complete vocational trade-training courses involving as much as a thousand hours of instruction (as was the case in the dental-technician, mortuary-science, dietetics, and nursing courses). Other courses taken by dropouts involved up to four hundred hours of class instruction, excluding homework assignments. The sex of the trainee was not significantly related to the rate of trade-training-course completion, nor was the trainee's ethnic origin.

Regardless of the fact that the initial employment rate of these Lavanburg trainees was encouraging, they tended over time to be unable to retain their jobs. Unemployment occurred irrespective of whether the initial placement was related or unrelated to training. Nor was there any relation between course completion and employment stability.

On the basis of these data, one may conjecture that the training

[6] "Supplementary Report to the Lavanburg-Corner House Vocational Trade Training Experimental and Demonstration Project" (mimeographed, New York, Mobilization For Youth, August 31, 1964), pp. 2–3.

program is successful in carrying youngsters through training and into an initial job. But factors external to job training seem to be reflected in the smaller and smaller numbers of youngsters who are able to hold their positions.

Since the Lavanburg demonstration in 1963, more than four hundred Mobilization youths have received trade-school training.[7] From July 1966 to April 1967, there were ninety-five Mobilization trainees enrolled in various trade schools, fifty-eight on a full-time basis and thirty-seven on a part-time basis while working. Male and female enrollees were equal in number; 66 percent of the youngsters were high-school dropouts; 30 percent were Negro, 50 percent Puerto Rican, and 20 percent white. Of these ninety-five trade-school enrollees, sixty-one terminated their training before completion, and thirty-four successfully finished their course work. The reasons given for terminating trade training by the sixty-one trainees who did so are as follows:

> Twenty-five secured work that was related to their training.
> Eleven secured work that was unrelated to their training.
> Five trainees returned to Mobilization to work in a crew or dispersed job.
> Three trainees returned to MFY through counselor contact and were classed as in counseling.
> Seventeen trainees had no further record of contact with MFY.

The rate of successful completion of trade training was inversely related to the length of time the course took—the longer the course, the fewer trainees finished. In addition, whether a trainee had completed high school seems to be a determinant of his ability to hold a job, especially for males. For example, males and females who completed high school did equally well in the number of jobs held, percentage of time employed, and percentage of time in employment related to training. Male dropouts were more severely penalized then female dropouts in these respects. The male dropout does poorest in employment.

The school status of a trainee was not an important correlate in

[7] Seventy-three in 1963, 116 in 1964, 45 in 1965, 121 in 1966, and 48 in 1967.

either course completion or initial placement. Thus, although it was possible to guide the male dropout, through training, persuade him to finish training, and then place him on a job, male dropouts, even those with a high level of motivation like this population, tend to become unemployed. The reasons for this deserve intensive research.

Direct Placement

Candidates for direct placement include persons from several different categories: graduates of MFY work-training programs who have developed appropriate work attitudes and vocational skills; applicants for MFY services whose attitudes and skills warrant immediate employment and who consequently can bypass training; and applicants who are not equipped for the labor market but who are so intent on immediate employment that they will not tolerate the necessary counseling and training services. The experience of the agency indicates that only about 10 percent of the applicants who applied to the program initially had sufficient skills to be placed on a job in which there was some chance of advancement and opportunity for promotion.

An employment office for youth is by itself not particularly effective or useful. Placements from such an agency would generally be of short duration and would entail a very high turnover. Lack of basic English and arithmetic skills, poor work habits, unrealistic expectations, unavailability of sufficient entry-level jobs which promise advancement, and a variety of personal and social problems, as noted in detail in other chapters, make the placement of most low-income youth, especially those eighteen and under, a difficult and costly operation.

It is clear from the Mobilization experience not only that a majority of low-income youths need training prior to placement on a job, but also that, once placed on a job, the trainee must be followed up.[8] While direct placement of applicants is probably the cheapest form of employment service in the short run, in the long

[8] As noted in other chapters, training is most effective when there is the prospect of an actual job at the conclusion of training. Job-placement and job-development services are as important as training itself.

run it is the most costly—not only to the trainees themselves, but also to the employers who hire these youngsters and to the economy in general, which has lost the opportunity of adding to the skilled portion of its labor force.

5

A Demonstration Prevocational Program

Fred Lorber

The difficulty in organizing a prevocational training program lies in identifying a group of clients with similar employability problems. An exception is the recent arrivals from Puerto Rico who speak little or no English. Their basic problems are not only English-language deficiency (communicating and reading) but also acculturation difficulties, which can be further specified in such categories as health, diet, grooming, knowledge of city geography and transportation, understanding local employment customs, the need for security and a feeling of welcome, etc.

During 1962–63, special consideration was given, within the normal structure of the Division of Employment Opportunities, to Puerto Rican youngsters who were inarticulate and illiterate in English. Bilingual receptionists, employment counselors, and crew chiefs were employed. The Education Division was called in to give on-the-job English classes in several of the subsidized work projects, and youngsters were encouraged to attend special English classes offered in the evening.

Trainees who were not literate in English got on well in sheltered workshops with Spanish-speaking crew chiefs, When they were upgraded to on-the-job training or placement in private employment, they were again confronted not only with language difficulties but also with their unfamiliarity with the style of life in metropolitan New York. It became clear that language deficiency was not the only problem and that something new was needed for these young people.

A special program was designed for these recent arrivals and launched in 1964. The program selects trainees who have had minimal experience with the difficulties of living and job hunting in New York, and deals with them as a homogeneous group. Supervisory personnel work as a team in planning and group leadership; they try to cut through the youngsters' feelings of isolation by dealing in depth with their problems of language and acculturation, utilizing the values of group interaction.

The key elements of the program have been as follows: a program coordinator of Puerto Rican descent with skill in establishing warm and intimate relations with her clients; a staff trained under the coordinator's guidance; a group-counseling and work approach that fosters esprit de corps; the teaching of basic English commuication skills, using curriculum materials developed to meet individual intellectual and employment needs; and job placement based upon the training, ability, and potential of each youngster.

Over the years the structure of the program has undergone change, new ideas have emerged, and the division itself has shifted emphasis. Sixty-seven enrollees participated in the program before the start of the research experiment in 1965. They were Puerto Rican males who spoke little or no English, had been residents of New York City not more than one and a half years, and were seventeen to twenty-one years old when they entered the program. They were treated in three successive groups; twenty began in September 1964, twenty in December 1964, and twenty-seven in May 1965.

The original design, which was applied to the first two groups of enrollees, divided the six-month program into three phases.

Phase 1: Enrollees functioned for three months in two crews of ten, each having half-days of English instruction, field trips, and discussions, and half-days of work training in a special construction crew. The two crews alternated activities; one worked under a bilingual crew chief while the other was in class. The coordinator held daily group-counseling sessions and scheduled individual counseling as needed. She also met regularly with the teacher and crew chief.

Phase 2: To wean the youths from dependence on their special groups, they were assigned individually to regular work-training

crews but continued to receive counseling and remediation tailored
to their needs. Most of the youths were excused from the last half
hour of work so that they could attend English classes held daily
from 3:00 to 4:30 P.M.

Phase 3: The youths were upgraded into full-time crew training, on-the-job training, or if they were ready, private employment.
The program's coordinator maintained close contact with them
after placement.

After six months' experience operating the program, the division
staff revised it for the third group, those entering in May 1965.
Phase 1 became a six-week, introductory period of orientation, intensive counseling, and instruction in English and arithmetic fundamentals. At its close, enrollees' academic level and training
preferences were assessed. During Phase 2 they were each assigned
to several training crews instead of being restricted to a single
work experience. For remedial work they were divided into two
sections according to their language achievement. After six months
of work experience, they entered Phase 3 for job placement or
upgrading.

The coordinator of the program was responsible for all activities. She met with the group daily, met individual members of the
group regularly, and planned field trips and other special programs
such as a parents' committee, parties celebrating holidays, and
significant dates within the program itself. The remedial instructor
and the crew chief of the building-repair project for the first two
groups were also bilingual and were specially selected for their
ability to reach the type of youngster in the program, in the hope
that they would become role models for them. New education materials were developed that, it was hoped, would be intelligible and
appealing to Puerto Rican youngsters.

The program was quite successful. By July 1965, more than two
thirds of the first two groups had found jobs or were still in training six to nine months after initial enrollment.[1] Moreover, the only
program with a higher success rate was the Hospital Training Program, for female high-school graduates. The dropout rate from the
special program was unusually low. Of the total enrollment of

[1] The chapter in this volume on "An Appraisal of Youth Employment
Programs" discusses the difficulties of precisely defining criteria of success.

sixty-seven, only ten had dropped out. Five of these had moved away; two had found jobs on their own; one had had to be dismissed; and contact had been lost for unspecified reasons with the remaining two trainees.

Weekly crew-chief ratings indicated that every youngster who completed the first two phases (six months) of training clearly became more proficient in the general use of tools and increased his productive capacity. The development of healthy attitudes toward work and training was at first impeded by a few participants who had been in New York longer and had already acquired a tough veneer and blasé attitude. At first they tried to "wise up" the newer boys. However, with the support of the staff the newer boys were able to resist these negative pressures. In fact, using the cohesiveness of the group as a lever, the program coordinator was able to pull marginal members into line with a shape-up-or-ship-out ultimatum.

The boys in the program obviously dressed better than they had before, and many of them gained weight by following the dietary recommendations of the program coordinator. They responded enthusiastically to field trips and films used to familiarize them with New York City and its inhabitants.

Significant results were obtained in the area of English literacy as indicated by the test scores. For example, among the first twenty youngsters, eleven were originally non-English-speaking (three of whom were also illiterate in Spanish), six had scant English ability, and three were reading at the fifth-grade level. All but three improved on the retests; in the three-month period the average gain was 1.4 grades.

Of the seventeen youngsters in the first group who were retested on the Woody-McCall Arithmetic Test, twelve showed improvement, two remained at the same level, and three dropped slightly. The average improvement was 1.6 grades. Groups 2 and 3 showed similar results.

In the summer of 1965 the six-month tooling-up period for the controlled experiment began. No provision had been made by the funding sources for a special program of the sort described; however, an agreement was negotiated with the Neighborhood Youth Corps in December of that year to set aside thirty job slots for a special pretraining program for Puerto Rican recent arrivals. In order to serve the growing number of youths who needed this kind of programming, without handicapping the design of the experiment, it was decided to assign youngsters first to this special program for six weeks (subsequently increased to ten weeks).[2] The program consisted essentially of intensive remedial instruction in English speaking and reading. Also, female trainees were included in the program for the first time.

Those youngsters who entered Neighborhood Youth Corps crew training after the ten weeks of pretraining instruction were reassigned to counselors in charge of the crews; youngsters who entered dispersed training or who bypassed training and were placed on jobs remained under the supervision of their special program counselors. As Neighborhood Youth Corps funding became more flexible, enrollment in the ten-week program increased to forty-five youngsters, and the staff increased to three vocational counselors, three teachers, and a program aide in addition to the coordinator.

The foundation of warmth and acceptance is laid immediately for each new enrollee at his initial interview with the program coordinator. The walls of the coordinator's small office contain a blackboard listing the names of all youngsters currently in the ten-week program according to their class-counselor groups, a large chart depicting many of the important people in Puerto Rico's history as well as a map of the island, and, scattered about the walls, pictures of former enrollees in military attire, with their new wives or husbands or children, pictures of monuments in Puerto Rico, Spain, and New York, and postcards and various other mementos from former enrollees.

The room as well as the initial interview serves to welcome the new enrollee to a new phase in his young life. Nor is he the first person like himself to embark on this challenge. The trainee will return many times to this room where his name is on the blackboard, and each time he will be welcomed with salutations and expressions of delight at his most recent achievements.

At the initial interview the coordinator tries to discover any special problems or anxieties, and she determines the youngster's

[2] The research design is described in the chapter on "Overview of Employment Opportunities" in this volume.

conversational level in English. He is then assigned to a counselor and an English class. He will probably meet his counselor and report to class on the same day.

There are three classroom groups, each with its own counselor. The lowest reading and conversation group is composed mostly of trainees who are illiterate in English and who have less than a seventh-grade reading level in Spanish. This class has the youngsters with the most serious problems. Often the failure to have learned to speak English and/or to read Spanish can be traced to physical problems, such as sight or speech defects, or to emotional problems, such as extreme shyness or anxiety. It is not unusual to discover that youngsters who had been judged mentally retarded, by conventional testing methods, are actually suffering from physical or emotional disorders which can be overcome with the proper care and positive reinforcement.

The second or intermediate group is composed of trainees who have had some high-school education and are fairly literate in Spanish although they speak almost no English. The third group is composed primarily of high-school graduates who are literate in Spanish and capable of learning English comparatively fast. About 25 percent of all program enrollees fall into this group. They present their own special problems. They are generally well-motivated, intelligent, and ambitious, but handicapped by their inability to speak English. Employment opportunities commensurate with the ambitions of these youngsters are hard to come by.

Each class meets daily from 9:00 A.M to noon and again from 1:00 to 4:00 P.M. Once each week the counselor meets with the group for an hour or so. At least once a week, the entire program membership meets with the program coordinator as well. At this meeting the coordinator reviews her acquaintance with the trainees and make announcements about employment and training opportunities. Usually some cultural or social activity climaxes this meeting. On Fridays classes are let out early so the youngsters can cash their checks and the entire staff can meet in the coordinator's office for discussion. Each program member is mentioned individually. Special attention is devoted to new members, to those about to terminate the ten-week program and move into a work-training area, and to those who have had personal problems.

The coordinator also meets individually with each staff member to work out strategies concerning job placement, tutoring, or the personal problems of particular trainees. Counselors usually see each youngster privately during the week; however, when the situation calls for it, they may see certain youngsters daily. The time a young man spends in the classroom or with the counselor, as well as the time the staff spends discussing and planning for him, depends entirely upon the needs and problems of the individual.

The implicit goal of the program is to help each youngster become a secure and intelligent adult with a sense of personal dignity and value. The primary means to this goal are personal attention and the fostering of group support and pride. The formal objectives of the program are acculturation, remedial education, and job placement.

A reading lesson in the classroom will, for example, have as its subject matter United States history, or the tools of a carpenter or seamstress; while the lesson is progressing, the teacher constantly reinforces the skills and development of individual members. Observers cannot help but notice the constant flow of encouragement and positive reinforcement in the classrooms, the counselor's offices, and the coordinator's office. Every improvement is celebrated, each setback is quickly absorbed by the staff and put into its proper perspective. For many youngsters this is the first time they have ever received such personal attention.

Some observers have been critical of this approach and have characterized it as Momism, predicting that youngsters will become so dependent upon the program that they will never leave it. The results belie such predictions. For example, many graduates of this program have gone into Job Corps programs all over the country with great success. Many who return to Puerto Rico or move away from the neighborhood establish mature, intelligent relationships with the program staff via the mails and occasional visits. Once a youngster has left the program and gone out on his own, he seldom returns except as a friend; few former clients need continued help.

The research staff is planning an extensive evaluation of this program. The service staff, though, is already convinced that this is an excellent model for an orientation program. While this program has been quite successful in holding onto clients and motivating them to learn, the question remains whether the program can be adapted for other disadvantaged groups such as Negro adolescents, delinquent or criminal youth, non-English-speaking adults, etc. It may be that the approach is useful only for recent arrivals from Puerto Rico who have not been subjected to the pressures of the slum environment that militate against successful involvement in training programs, such as delinquent peer groups and repeated failures in school and work experiences. Should this be the case, the approach would still be useful for the new immigrant as it offers an alternative for the socialization provided by the slum.

6

Vocational Counseling of Trainees

Harold H. Weissman and Burton Weinstein

"Constancy, energy, perseverance, industry, patience, accuracy, cherefulness, hope, self-denial, self-respect, power of good example, and nobility of character"—this was the formula offered to the job seeker by the "success" literature of the late nineteenth century. Along with books of general "uplift," such volumes as *The Boy's Book of Trades and the Tools Used in Them* (1886) were written specifically to assist young men in choosing and preparing themselves for a vocation.

Around the turn of the century it began to be suggested that what the young needed most was not advice on the value of honesty, industry, and thrift, but the plain facts about the various occupations, particularly the new ones: their advantages and drawbacks, how to enter and how to advance in them, and other practical and specific information.

In 1908, Frank Parsons, a professor at Boston University, founded the Vocational Bureau of Boston. This was the beginning of modern vocational guidance as a movement and discipline. The early vocational counselors were concerned mainly with finding the right job for the right man. They saw themselves essentially as bridges between men and jobs.

In recent years, vocational counseling has taken on therapuetic and rehabilitative aspects. The vocational problems of clients are viewed not only in terms of finding the right job but also in terms of helping the client to overcome the physical or emotional handicaps that limit his employability. Thus, vocational counselors at

Mobilization aimed not only to place a trainee at a job in which he could find permanent employment and a chance of advancement but also to help him to develop positive work habits and attitudes, to move ahead with his education, to increase his self-esteem, to improve his capacity to establish meaningful relationships with adults and his ability to cope with problems on his job.

All this was to be achieved by establishing a helping relationship with trainees. Beginning at intake and continuing through training in the crew or dispersed work, and finally at job placement and follow-up, the counselor was to offer assistance in solving the inevitable work-related problems that the trainee would face.

Role Problems

The job of vocational counselor is a frustrating one, given the broad motivational and vocational goals many counselors have had at Mobilization. The practice of making the counselor responsible for a trainee from the moment he enters the agency until after he is placed on a job requires that the counselor possess a wide range of expertise. Few could meet this requirement. Herman and Sadofsky list the skills and capacities which such counselors should have:

> In addition to those [tasks] he must undertake in the intake process, his task may include counseling youth during training; assessing a trainee's progress to determine when transfer to another activity or referral to placement is indicated; observing trainees at the work site and working closely with the foreman; instructing the youth in job and training possibilities, placement problems, preparation for job interviews, forms and tests, and conventional behavior on the job; instructing youth in various aspects of community living such as the geography of the community, its transportation and other services, unemployment insurance, social security, workmen's compensation, withholding taxes, contracts, leases, and installment buying; preparing training plans for youth in cooperation with employers, school personnel, the Bureau of Apprenticeship and Training, and others; working closely with job-development specialists in order to keep trainees informed about labor-market opportunities and requirements; helping to prepare employers to receive youth; aiding in job development and placement; counsel-

ing youth who have been placed in private employment or who have returned to school; supervising the activities of interns, graduate students, and other volunteers; interceding with legal authorities, welfare department, and other agencies on behalf of the trainee; recording pertinent data and progress notes on all individuals in his caseload; and being available at least two evenings each week at the work program center.[1]

When the employment program began in October 1962, the vocational counselors had the central coordinating role. Each trainee was to have his own counselor who would guide him through the various aspects of the program. Clients were to be assigned to counselors on a random basis. In devising this program strategy, the value of continuity of service, which seemed to be inherent in the one-to-one counselor/client relationship, was preeminent. Since it was known that counselors came from different orientations and backgrounds—some from employment agencies, others from rehabilitation agencies, others from vocational testing—it was anticipated that some of the potential values of specialization would be lost by having only one counselor assigned to a trainee throughout the trainee's stay in the program.

Within a half year after the program went into operation, it became apparent that a high percentage of trainees were remaining in the work crews and were not moving on to regular jobs. A survey of the case loads revealed that those counselors who came from a rehabilitation background were keeping their clients in work crews. Those who came from employment-service and placement backgrounds tended to move their clients into jobs more quickly. The placement-oriented counselors tended to view locating a job as the most important service the program could offer, while the rehabilitation-oriented counselors tended to view the training and experiences in the training situation as the important program ingredients.

The survey also indicated that the rates of successful job placements made by training- and job-oriented counselors were not appreciably different.[2] A year after the program began operation,

[1] Melvin Herman and Stanley Sadofsky, *Youth-Work Programs* (New York, New York University Graduate School of Social Work, 1966), p. 124.

[2] Success criteria were, in fact, rather crude. It may be that the administrators read more into the survey than was warranted.

in late 1963, a separate intake section was set up. This section had the responsibility of determining whether a trainee was ready for immediate job placement or needed prior experience in work crew. Rehabilitation-oriented counselors now had responsibility for applicants only after intake processing. The first break was made in counselor responsibility for continuity of service from entry to exit.

At the same time, placement-oriented counselors were given the responsibility for handling only those youngsters judged ready for placement by the intake workers. Thus the placement-oriented counselors became in effect job developers and placement specialists. These changes, however, did not resolve the problem of the training-oriented counselors' holding trainees for long periods of time in the work crews. A six-month limit on training was introduced, but this procedure was not effective, for the maximum stay tended to become the minimum stay. Furthermore, exceptions were constantly being requested. To counter the problem, the placement-oriented counselors, who were in effect carrying out only placement functions, were finally given joint responsibility for placement counseling during the sixth month of a trainee's work-crew experience. This policy was effective in moving trainees more rapidly out of training and also served as a further differentiation of counselor duties, since the rehabilitation-oriented counselors would be responsible for counseling only trainees in training. Once the trainee was placed on a job, he became the responsibility of the placement counselor.

In late 1965, a further realignment was made. Instead of receiving trainees from the intake section, counselors were assigned to specific crews. This shift, the final one made, further specialized their work. The counselor initially had the primary responsibility for guiding a trainee's career at Mobilization; by the end the counselor was one of several persons involved in this process. Specialization did have the effect of freeing counselors to spend more time with trainees. Yet an average case load at Mobilization has varied from thirty to fifty active cases, and the possibility of spending a great deal of time developing a helping relationship is certainly constrained. In a work week of thirty-five hours, a counselor may be able to spend only fifteen to twenty hours actively engaged with his clients. He may have to locate missing checks, fill out a myriad

number of forms and reports, make referrals for the clients to
medical and other services, appear in court, etc.

As one counselor noted:

> When I get an hour with a kid, that's a luxury. The job demands
> time which doesn't exist. Sometimes you'll have to beat around the
> bush three or four times before a kid tells you what's bothering
> him. Depth counseling under these conditions is a myth. Many of
> us have to manage the situations that arise in a superficial way.
> We try to get a kid going okay, and then we hope that he'll *keep*
> going okay.

Another factor which makes the job of a counselor difficult is
the problem of determining precisely what the factors are that are
inhibiting the client's vocational success and dealing with them.
Although approximately 10 percent of the trainees who came to
the program were severely disturbed emotionally or handicapped
in other ways, a considerably larger percentage present an attitudinal picture of poor motivation, a fantastic lack of information
about the job world, and a great misperception of Mobilization itself and its training program. Much of what the counselor needs in
order to deal with these problems is not under his control. For
example, the time the trainee is willing to spend with the counselor
is crucial. When they see a counselor for the first time, many Mobilization youngsters will present him with some insoluble problem or demand: "Get me a certain job," "I need this or that
amount of money," "Get me a job today, I need one quick." This
demand is a test. The client is sizing the counselor up: "Is he a
threat to me? Will he put me down? What can I get out of him?
Can he pay off?" The counselor is, in effect, the person who is
being directed, and he must pay off immediately. If he cannot deliver a job, then he must deliver a realistic and meaningful alternative that the trainee can understand. If the counselor cannot
deliver, the trainee may not return.

Ultimately, the counselor must be able to produce jobs that the
clients want and like. At Mobilization this has not always been
possible. First, a wide variety of jobs suitable for and attractive to
every client has not been available. Often trainees have had to wait
for a long time, and this has further strained the counselor-trainee

relationship. During this limbo period the client may find himself strapped for funds, he may get into trouble with the police, or he might be having family troubles. Normally his counselor should be able to assist him with these difficulties, but the client might be too busy seeking a job or too disillusioned to discuss these things wth his counselor.

If a counselor is able to place his client on a job or in a training crew, he must make an attempt to keep him there or move him to another job if necessary. It is the counselor's responsibility to keep in touch with his client, to monitor his growth in the job, and to step in before client-employer friction gets out of hand. The employer's attitude is crucial and at times not controllable. Many employers will contact counselors when they sense trouble, but others don't recognize signs of trouble or don't care. At times Mobilization has attempted to keep a file on each employer and how he treated trainees, but this is a difficult and time-consuming task, and other tasks have priority.

Certain structural problems have also made the counselor's job difficult. For example, when trainees are assigned to dispersed work outside the agency, it is much more difficult for a counselor to see them either during crises or more casually. Likewise, the counselor has not always been completely free to deal with trainees on the basis of what he considers best for them. At times, for example, the agency has been committed to filling a certain number of Neighborhood Youth Corps jobs, and counselors, though not required to channel applicants toward these jobs, were still under a certain amount of pressure to see them filled.

Perhaps the most difficult problem for the counselor is the passivity and seeming disinterest of the applicants. Some seem to exhibit a chronic feeling of defeat. Some applicants are so sure they will fail on the job that they will not go when they are sent. They "can't find the place" or they "didn't like the place"—a place they have never seen.

As one counselor noted, vocational choice or direction of clients is usually based on nonoccupationally related criteria. To provide only occupational information and exposure as a means of developing realistitc decision making is naïve, yet the counselor felt limited in his ability to help trainees with these nonoccupational factors:

> To want to and be able to consider alternatives presupposes minimal knowledge of oneself, a fairly positive attitude toward oneself, some confidence and investment in one's future (based in large part on love and concern for oneself), and a desire for change —in short, ego strength and an ability to project oneself into the future. This stands in sharp contrast to the hesitant, frightened adolescent, conditioned to failure, who will slide with a sigh of dependent relief into almost any training situation which will give him a paycheck and an illusion of making an effort at being a success.

Group counseling seemed to offer a way of dealing with many of these problems. At times it is simply the situation that frustrates the trainee and the counselor. Youthfulness and inexperience create difficulties. For example, James M. showed great promise when he was in Mobilization's auto shop. He had a police record involving auto theft and was nearing the end of his parole period. His counselor got him a job as a mechanic, but he was cautioned not to drive a car as a condition of his parole. James worked on the job for a number of months, but although he was top dog in Mobilization's shop, to his superior he was just another mechanic. James became bored with his routine work, but he never mentioned this to his counselor. He wanted to quit, but he didn't want to let his counselor or his former crew chiefs down. Finally he took a customer's car, without authorization and in direct violation of his parole, and went for a joy ride. He was fired immediately.

Group counseling might have helped James. It did Bill who had similarly difficult problems.[3]

> Bill, age twenty, had a tendency to react aggressively to authority. (Through discussion in the group he began to see how he reacted, especially when the other members pointed out his reactions to

[3] Because of the nature of the research design, even though group counseling seemed a promising technique, it could not be introduced into all aspects of the program until the conclusion of the experiment in 1968. Abraham Helfand, "Group Counseling as an Approach to the Work Problems of Disadvantaged Youth," *Rehabilitation Counseling Bulletin*, Vol. II (December 1967), p. 114.

him.) He was hired as a stockroom worker at the same rate of pay as a more experienced worker, who acted as the foreman. The foreman resented this, and Bill felt that he was given all "the heavy and dirty stuff" to do as a result. Because Bill wanted to keep the job, he expected that he would have to take it from the foreman at the beginning, but hoped that he could get along with him after a while. After three weeks he finally spoke to his employer about the situation. By this time Bill had demonstrated that he was a hard worker and could take orders. The employer appraised the situation and corrected it by talking it over with the foreman. Bill himself expressed great surprise that he could talk to an employer with such success. He had acquired one more tool—and an effective one—that he could use in the future in his effort to maintain employment.

Conclusion

Vocational counseling as a field has not precisely defined its methods and techniques into a coherent body of knowledge. In general, the training of counselors was not suited to the needs of the trainee population at Mobilization—trainees who know almost nothing of the labor market, have poor work attitudes, and a host of personal and social problems. The difficulties counselors faced were exacerbated by the periodic shift in emphasis of the total employment program to meet new understandings of how best to deal with the trainee population.

There is little doubt that trainees benefit from individual attention. Although initially it was felt this would result from assigning each trainee to one counselor who would oversee his total career in the program, experience proved that freeing counselors from intake and job-development tasks and assigning them to specific work areas allowed for more individual attention to trainees. It also allowed counselors to become more familiar with the work-crew situations and labor-market conditions in their area of specialization.

It seems extremely unlikely that in a work-training program such as that of MFY, which stresses the training of large numbers of youths, there will be sufficient time and proper conditions available for counselors to attain their goals solely on a one-to-one basis. Essentially the job of a vocational counselor at MFY involved dealing with all the problems that inhibit trainees in their efforts to complete training and hold a job. To achieve this goal, counselors need not restrict themselves to a one-to-one relationship.[4] Organizing discussion groups of trainees to offer mutual support on especially stressful points in training—e.g., placement on the first real job—or helping trainees organize a union in which occupational information could be exchanged are examples of other techniques.

Although the majority of MFY's trainees had difficulties related to motivation and attitude, it does not necessarily follow that these problems should be dealt with solely, or even primarily, through vocational counseling on an individual or a group basis. The solution to such problems, to the extent that they are solvable by a program such as MFY's, are related to such noncounseling factors as the availability of a job following training, the potentiality for fun and sociability in the work or training situation, the availability of ancillary resources such as remedial education or health services, and the like—in short, the total structure of the program. The total structure of an employment program must support the counselor in his efforts; the counselor cannot substitute for a faulty structure.

[4] In 1968 a new plan for vocational counseling was developed at MFY, utilizing group counseling to help trainees learn job-related skills rather than simply to deal with problems of work adjustment. "New Directions in Counseling at Mobilization For Youth" (mimeographed, New York, Mobilization For Youth, 1968).

7

Remedial Education In a Work-Training Program

Burton Weinstein

Aside from his lack of specific job skills, the typical Mobilization trainee was severely handicapped by his educational limitations. In the clerical area, for example, almost 50 percent of the trainees who were referred for private employment were not hired, and the overwhelming majority of these were rejected because of their poor academic background. Their English skills were poor; they could not do the arithmetic believed necessary for the job; they could not score well enough on the employer's preemployment tests. Although clerical work, of course, demands a relatively good academic background, even trainees referred to jobs in the manual trades were often not hired because of such deficiencies.

Most trainees entered the work program with serious educational gaps; many were also deficient in their command of spoken English. Some of the Puerto Rican-born trainees had sufficient language skill to manage work and educational tasks in an English-speaking culture, but there are others whose proficiency was so limited that they could not engage in sustained everyday conversation or begin to achieve reading competence in English. Even those trainees whose native language is English were generally severely limited in the fundamental tool skills, with reading and arithmetic achievement scores between the third- and fifth-grade levels. Many had a skill level so low that they could be described as functional nonreaders; a few could handle reading and arithmetic tasks at a relatively high level of difficulty (sixth grade or above).

Of the trainees in the work program from July 1965 to June 1966, 13 percent had only a seventh-grade education or less. The median schooling completed was ninth grade. Only 22 percent were high-school graduates. Many of those who applied for service in the work program may be considered long-term dropouts in much the same sense as their fathers represent the long-term unemployed. More than half of the trainees had been out of school for at least a year at the time of their applications, and one third of the dropouts had left school for reasons related to poor academic performance.

Figures showing the formal grade level reached before these youngsters dropped out of school may be misleading, for in many cases, the grade level in no way represents the academic level the individual achieved. Of the group as a whole, almost half (49 percent) were below fifth-grade level in arithmetic and only 21 percent were at sixth-grade level or above. One third of the English-speaking clients were reading below the fifth-grade level, and this group included 8 percent below the third-grade level. Table I shows the grade level and test scores of twenty-one randomly selected trainees.

TABLE I. GRADE, READING, AND ARITHMETIC LEVELS
(21 randomly selected trainees)

Formal grade level completed	*Graded reading level (Gates score)*	*Graded arithmetic level (W.R.A. score)*
HSG	7.9	5.5
HSG	4.1	5.6
11	9.6	6.9
11	8.9	5.9
11	6.7	5.6
11	Nonreader in Eng.	5.4
10	7.6	4.9
10	6.5	4.1
10	4.5	4.4
10	3.8	4.4
10	3.3	4.4
10	2.8	3.8

Formal grade level completed	Graded reading level (Gates score)	Graded arithmetic level (W.R.A. score)
9	10.3	5.2
9	6.9	5.9
9	3.7	5.8
9	2.9	4.4
9	2.5	4.5
8	6.7	6.7
8	6.0	5.5
8	4.7	5.0
3	Nonreader in Eng.	3.6

The Mobilization For Youth Remedial Education Program was established "to help sixteen- to twenty-one-year-old trainees in the Neighborhood Youth Corps overcome their deficits in English language skills, reading, and mathematics" as well as "to improve their capacity for problem-solving and self-instruction." The idea of a work-training program with an educational component is not unique to Mobilization. Training programs have recognized the academic deficiencies of their target populations, and most large-scale programs have incorporated some sort of remedial education in an attempt to deal with the problem. These educational components tend to reflect the philosophy of the program of which they are a part. Thus, the education curriculum of a program that attempts to teach specific job-related skills may center around the work itself. There may be a general Three R curriculum as well, but often it will be a complement to the main effort. Work-orientation programs, on the other hand, tend to stress reading and communication skills rather than the educational requirements for any particular job or group of jobs. The reading deficiency that characterizes most clients of work-orientation programs is too great to overcome by a short-term exposure to remediation.[1] Work-orientation training programs have generally dealt inadequately with functional illiteracy because there has been insufficient time to effect any real change.

---

[1] *Youth Employment Programs in Perspective* (Washington, D.C., Department of Health, Education and Welfare, 1965), p. 84.

Voluntary Attendance

Mobilization's work-training program has always had an educational component, but its form has undergone several changes. When the training program first got under way, the education program was part of Mobilization's Division of Educational Opportunities, whose major concern was innovation in the public-school system. The remedial program was given low priority and was regarded as a service to the Employment Division. The program was run on a voluntary basis; trainees attended only if they wanted to do so, and they received no payment for attendance. The classes were devoted to reading and arithmetic, and were held during the evening hours, after the trainees' working day was finished. Voluntary attendance led to heterogeneous classes. The class size also could not be controlled—teachers never knew whether only three or four trainees would show up, or as many as eighteen or twenty. Teachers were virtually on their own and often had to devise their own teaching material.

The counselors tried to persuade their clients to attend these classes, but they were never very successful, and the program rarely had more than eighty trainees enrolled on an active basis. This was not surprising; it is not realistic to expect a youngster to volunteer for an education program that may rekindle his old anxieties and set him up for still another round of academic failure. Furthermore, trainees who enrolled in the Neighborhood Youth Corps to improve their employment opportunities often found it difficult to understand or accept the logic of participating in a school-type program as part of work training. A survey of 226 trainees who were exposed to this voluntary education program revealed that, although many were aware of their academic deficiencies, they either refused to attend the classes at all or attended sporadically. "I know about them but I don't need them" was not an unusual response from trainees who had been denied access to jobs because of their poor English, spelling, speech, and arithmetic.

Education at the Training Site

In 1964 the voluntary program was altered. The director of the Employment Opportunities Division felt that the program should have its own education component, one that would be tied directly to the training sites and under the control of the work-corps staff.

Bringing education directly to the work sites proved to be a difficult task. The device of roving teachers who would visit each work site was difficult to coordinate with training demands and work flow. The use of the crew chiefs as teachers was dependent on the talents of men who were hired for their ability as craftsmen, not because they could teach reading skills. Perhaps most serious of all, education interfered with the work, and the experience of work was what most staff members felt was crucial.

With the failure of the attempt to bring education to the work sites, the agency changed its tack. Remedial education was going to be based on the Three R's and not necessarily geared to work or training. This was a far-from-easy change of direction for the work program to take, and the question of work-based versus skills-based education was never settled adequately.

The redirection of the education program in 1965 coincided with the beginning of the research program,[2] intended to determine whether a part-work, part-education program will result in improved academic skills and a better vocational outcome than a program which offers full-time work training with no educational component.

Required Remedial Education

The current research design calls for those trainees who are chosen at random to have education (approximately half) to receive a half day of work training and a half day of remedial education. In a training week of thirty hours, then, those assigned to the education track get a nominal fifteen hours of remedial instruction.[3]

[2] See the Chapter on "Overview of Employment Opportunities" in this volume for a discussion of the research design.

[3] The program was lodged administratively in the Division of Educational Opportunities. In addition to its director, staff included three supervisors, two math teachers, three reading clinicians, six general teachers, and three who specialized in teaching trainees from the clerical and auto shops. This staff was all college trained. There were in addition three teacher aides who came from the neighborhood and had a high-school education.

The general objectives of the education program have been specified as follows:

1. Improvement of the educational skills of trainees through the development of a program for remediation and continued education geared to each trainee's capacity.

2. Demonstration of the direct connection between work and education to the trainee.

3. Overcoming the trainee's negative responses to school-related tasks by creating a learning enrivonment that will encourage him to play a significant role in the educational experience. This objective implies certain guidelines for the remediation program: a) The trainee must at all times be in control of his learning process. b) The trainee must be given a share of the responsibility for his own remediation. c) The trainee must be given clear evidence that the instructor is working for the realization of the trainee's goals.

Instructional groupings were formed to recognize the significant differences in trainees' communication, reading, and arithmetic proficiency. Three levels of instruction were available: *The English-Language Workshop* designed for trainees who speak little or no English; trainees assigned to this class could not understand a simple interview conducted in English. *The Communication Skills Workshop* intended for trainees who could understand spoken English but whose reading ability was below the fourth grade level on the Gates Reading Survey; generally this means that the trainee could not read material such as the New York *Daily News*. Finally, *Skills Station Classes* designed for trainees who demonstrated that they could understand and speak English, and whose reading level was above the 4.0 grade level.

These classes were further divided into three groups: fourth- to sixth-grade reading level, sixth grade and above, and a special class for those trying to get a high-school equivalency diploma. The fourth-grade reading level was selected as the minimal criterion for these classes, because it was felt that this is the point at which the ability to read becomes a useful tool in the acquisition of further knowledge.

One of the significant differences between Mobilization's classes and public-school classes was size. Mobilization's classes were limited to seven trainees in the language and communication workshops, and eleven in the skills station classes. Some classes further had the advantage of a Vista volunteer as well as a teacher.

Unlike the public schools, the remedial-education program offered learning experiences that were selected and programmed to guarantee the trainee immediate success. The whole focus of the program was on making the trainee aware that he is capable of learning and giving him the self-confidence that comes from knowing that he can learn. The problem of a trainee's self-image is probably the most difficult one that the teachers faced. Many of the trainees seem to have been convinced by previous failures in school that it is impossible for them to learn anything. The program operated on the assumption that, once they believe in their ability to learn, they will then start to learn.

Since the class size is so small, a teacher is able to stay with a trainee until he is able to return a satisfactory answer. There is no badgering, and a trainee rarely lost face before his friends, classmates, or teacher. In one class, for example, the teacher told the trainees to write out some pattern sentences from memory. One boy who had great difficulty with proper word order copied the sentences from a piece of paper which he had apparently been keeping for such an occasion. The teacher, instead of berating him for cheating (the formal classroom reaction), told him that the important thing was to remember the sentence *pattern* correctly after the exercise, that that was what really counted.

The program was designed to involve the trainee to the maximum extent possible. For example, trainees are given a comprehensive battery of diagnostic tests to determine their strengths and weaknesses in spoken English, reading, and mathematics. The resulting trainee profile is given to the supervisor of the remedial-education program, who uses it, with the trainee's prospective teachers, to devise a provisional education plan for each trainee. The teacher goes over this profile with the trainee, explaining his areas of strength and weakness in detail. Together the teacher and the trainee construct a learning map in each subject, reflecting not only the trainee's immediate academic requirements but his social and vocational aspirations as well.

Often the discovery of an educational need has immediate and positive effect on the vocational experience. One trainee in Mobilization's woodworking shop was so severely retarded in reading that his reading test in English could not be scored. In addition, his reading level was having an adverse effect on his training. If his crew chief told him to use a two-inch brass woodscrew, the trainee was at a loss because he couldn't read the labels on the storage bins. He couldn't find tools because he was unable to recognize words such as "screwdriver," "ruler," "rip saw," etc. After becoming aware of his reading problem in the shop, his remedial teacher developed a sight vocabulary of basic shop tools and terminology for him. The trainee is now able to function quite well on his training site.

Although the division of the trainee population into three instructional groupings based on reading and language skills necessitates the use of three different delivery systems, there are common elements in all three systems. In each group themes relating to the trainee's life play a major part in the instructional program and an effort is made to encourage the trainee to use his work and life experiences to give meaning to the formalized set of teaching aids. For example, a mimeographed sheet of problems in division contains questions such as "You have just hit the numbers and feel good about it, so you want to treat your friends to a 15-cent beer. How many beers can you buy with the 90 cents in your pocket?"

To ensure adequate exposure to basic vocabulary and sentence patterns, material is at first presented in a highly structured manner. As the trainee gains greater control over his new language skills, the classroom themes shift more and more toward community life, social issues, and the job market. Trainees work first with generalized and structured materials but as they begin to master each skill they have a growing opportunity to develop the skill with materials and content of their own choosing.

Although Mobilization's teachers are supposed to follow a set delivery strategy, they can modify it when necessary. If, after a period of several weeks, the prescribed delivery system fails to get a trainee moving or motivated, the teacher is free to construct any teaching strategy that works.[4]

[4] The Remedial Program produced in mimeographed form a number of teaching materials for use in the classes: "Intake, Quick Screening and

Formal Objectives

A statistically significant difference, according to Mobilization's research design, is an increase of a full grade level in a trainee's reading and arithmetic scores after remediation. The success or failure of the remediation attempt is to be determined by the differences between trainees' scores on the initial tests and on retests. Yet, for many of the trainees enrolled in the program, progress may be at such a slow pace as to go unnoticed on a formal testing instrument.

Reynaldo F. was expelled from high school because he assaulted his teacher. He is sixteen years old, but when he came to Mobilization, he scored zero on the reading test. He could print his name only with difficulty. He was convinced that he was stupid and could not learn. After being in the training program for almost four months; he could read a ruler, tell time and tell what day of the month it is, and he could read and write his address. Progress, to be sure, but how is it measured?

A characteristic of Mobilization's work-training program is its inability to hold trainees over a long period of time; almost 50 percent of the trainees who are placed on a training site leave the program within four months, and after twelve months almost the whole population will have turned over.

If Mobilization's remedial-education program is to be deemed a success, it must realize a significant performance gain in about two hundred hours of instruction—the equivalent of forty days of school. And this time tends to be reduced further by absences, retesting time, counselor appointments, and the field trips that are part of the training day. The remedial-education program has been asked to deliver results which may be impossible; yet, regardless of the results of the experiment, the remedial-education staff has been able to reach this population. It has turned out trainees who can understand more, read more, and want to learn more. It may, however, be a failure by formal criteria.

Placement Reading Test with Manual of Instruction," "Some Recommendations for a Phonetics Program for Spanish-speaking Students," "The Remedial Education Program: A Description of Its Structure, Curriculum Design, Courses of Study and a Selected Sample of Tested Teaching Units."

   In the short period of time that MFY's training program holds a trainee, there are only two realistic goals: (1) to alter the trainee's belief that he is stupid, and (2) to establish the relationship of continuing education to job advancement. To ensure that these attitudinal changes and learning increments are permanent, the community must make the requisite schools of continuing education available.[5]

   Both program components—education and work training—must deal with the problem of motivation. It is likely that for school dropouts the experience with and the desire to hold a particular job will be the best motivator for continuing education, the best enhancer of his self-image and confidence. Relating education to job requisites is probably the best strategy to be employed.

---

[5] Preliminary analysis of data from the research study indicates the importance of education to job success. "Education, more consistently than any of the other demographic variables, affects all three aspects of employment in about the same way. Thus high-school graduates are more likely than nongraduates to be employed, and if employed, are both more likely to have 'above minimum skill' jobs and to take home at least $60 in earnings." Preliminary Research Findings: Report to Office of Special Manpower Programs (Washington, D.C., Department of Labor, September 1968), pp. 1, 21.

8

The Problem of Job Placement

Burton Weinstein

In reply to your inquiry, we have checked with his supervisor in our Pharmacy Division. He informs us that Mr. A. [a Mobilization trainee] is a trustworthy and very conscientious employee and his work is above reproach.

—Personnel director
Brooklyn-Cumberland Medical Center

They don't want to work. Come in late seven out of ten times. Then they'd sit in the back and listen to the radio and tap their feet. They didn't work. You do everything to pacify them, but what do they want? Blood.

—Unidentified employer

Mobilization's pipeline finally ends at the labor market—a market which may absorb trainees at one time and reject them at another. The success or failure of a trainee in the market is determined by a number of factors, many of them far beyond the ability of the trainee or the training agency to control or modify.

Although a trainee may be a statistic in an analysis of the labor market, he is employed by a firm not by a labor market. The hiring policies of an individual firm may reflect the biases and idiosyncrasies of the men who direct it, the desire to project a certain image, as well as the more objective needs of the firm. Thus factors unrelated to the trainee's qualifications often have great effect on his success in the labor market. When requirements are waived, as

99

occasionally happens, the firm's justification is generally economic. Employer subjectivity in hiring is pervasive and affects the whole working population; day laborer or university professor, all feel its impact. Unfortunately, those who feel it it most seem least suited to cope with it.

Discrimination and Placement

When a sample of Mobilization's trainees, most of them Negro or Puerto Rican, were asked if they thought that they were ever discriminated against in trying to find jobs, the overwhelming majority replied in the negatitve—and even those who thought they *had* experienced discrimination could not specify its precise nature. It is often difficult to pinpoint the operation of racial prejudice. Many employers are simply too sophisticated to reject an applicant flatly because he is Negro, Jewish, Puerto Rican, Chinese, or whatever, particularly if the applicant is referred by some nondiscriminatory public or private agency. It is very easy for an employer so inclined to discriminate simply by telling an applicant that the job is filled.

Many business organizations are intensely concerned with the image the firm projects and are reluctant therefore to hire "certain types" of people to work in even menial and back-office positions. This type of discrimination is much more difficult to ferret out than the overt variety, since the employer himself is often convinced that his behavior is reasonable and fair. A large Brooklyn bank, for example, refused to hire a Mobilization trainee as a stock clerk because, said a bank officer, he was not "what we consider promotable, and we will only hire people who we feel can move up in our organization. People expect this from us as an employer, and it is good for our employees too."

Skills Requirements and Testing

An employer's skills requirements for entry-level jobs often box out an applicant. These requirements are often a function of the relation between the supply of labor available to a firm and the quantity it demands or needs. If a trainee enters the market at a time when an employer's labor needs outstrip the available supply, the employer may dilute his entry requirements, and the trainee will be absorbed very quickly. By comparing the qualifications required when the labor market is slack and when it is tight, it is possible to estimate the degree to which job requirements have been overstated. For example, a firm that does commercial sewing for months displayed a sign advertising "operator wanted—experienced only." Suddenly the sign was changed to "operators wanted —immediate openings." The reason? This firm had just landed a substantial contract with the U. S. Army.

The use of various tests to screen job applicants has been a major stumbling block in Mobilization's attempts to place clients. The supervisor of Mobilization's job-development section tries to have these tests waived whenever possible. He has often been able to show that there is little connection between a specific test and the job in question, but most of his requests to waive a test have been turned down. A major airline, for example, offered to place a number of Mobilization trainees as baggage-handlers provided that they could pass four tests. Three of these tests were based on arithmetic computation and sentence construction at a level designed for graduates of academic high schools, although the median school years completed by those employed as baggage men in the transportation industries is 10.9.

Another firm was willing to try out Mobilization trainees as shipping clerks but required them to pass a preemployment test of clerical aptitude, arithmetic fundamentals, and basic vocabulary. Of the five clients who took the test during a one-month period, four scored very badly in all three areas; the fifth trainee, a Puerto Rican, had two marginally acceptable scores but failed the vocabulary test.

Are the requirements of these firms unreasonable? The New York State Department of Labor has described the duties and requirements generally associated with the job of "shipping clerk" as follows:

DUTIES: Receives merchandise; packs, seals, and labels cartons; addresses mail and packages; refers to parcel-post rate book and zone guide; operates postage meter; delivers mail and packages; may be required to use telephone and write messages.

REQUIREMENTS: High-school graduate preferred but not always required. Must be able to read and write English. Must pass physical and clerical examinations in most large companies.

The requirements for the baggage-handler job seem to be way out of line, but those for shipping clerk do not seem overstated—especially when compared with the requirements presented by the Employment Service as the industry norm.

Not all employers use preemployment tests to screen job applicants, but the larger firms are more likely to use some formal testing device, especially if they have separate personnel departments. The most common tests for clerical, typing, and stockroom jobs are the Minnesota Clerical Test and the Short Employment Test, both published by the Psychological Corporation. One employer, a steamship company, administers this test to all applicants for low-level clerical jobs and admitted that they often had trouble filling available jobs because the people who applied for these positions could not pass the test.

The firms offering jobs in factories, either as machine operators or general help, and in the automotive trades, as mechanic's helpers, garagemen, and auto-body repairmen, were less likely to use any type of formal test, in part because most of these firms are considerably smaller than those offering clerical jobs. The firms that did use formal tests in manual jobs most often employed the Purdue Pegboard, the S.E.T., and the Crawford Small Parts Dexterity Test. One employer, who produces transformers, uses the Crawford test to screen coil winders. He has given the test to ninety job applicants over a period of three years and has hired only two. Most of the informal testing done for manual jobs involves some aspect of the job itself—micrometer reading, automobile-parts nomenclature, basic shop arithmetic, use of hand and power tools, and the like.

If testing seems to erect a barrier, the height varies with the job classification, as Tables I and II indicate. Of 486 trainees referred to jobs in the clerical and manual areas, 30 percent of the applicants for manual jobs were not hired because of testing failures, while the corresponding figure in the clerical area was 52 percent.[1]

Of 261 clients referred for jobs as clerk-typists, general clerks, shipping clerks, mailroom clerks, and stock clerks, 142 (54 percent) were hired and started work, and 119 were not hired. All but thirteen were rejected because of inadequate skills.

TABLE I. REASONS FOR NOT HIRING CLERICAL TRAINEES

Failed typing test	21
Failed test (unspecified)	19
Poor English	18
Failed S.E.T.	17
Failed Minnesota Clerical	13
Failed spelling test	11
Not enough experience	7
Poor arithmetic	7
Too young	4
Poor references	2

Of 225 clients referred for jobs as machine operators and helpers, 177 (78 percent) were hired and started work, and forty-eight were not hired. All but eight of these rejects represent skill deficiencies.

TABLE II. REASONS FOR NOT HIRING MACHINE OPERATORS AND HELPERS

Failed test	15
Insufficient English	14
Not qualified (unspecified)	7
Poor arithmetic	4
Too young	4
Insufficient experience	3
Police record Y. O.	1

Work Habits and Attitudes

Part of the employability approach to training is posited on the idea that a trainee needs to have the proper attitudes toward work,

[1] This is a clear indication that trainees need help with how to take tests. Staff was of the opinion that fear of tests cause many to score lower than their true potential.

over and above whatever skills he might acquire in training, before
he can make any headway up the occupational ladder. These attitudes and habits concern the need for promptness in reporting for
work, calling in when sick, and other such time-oriented work
mores.

Employers are often willing to tolerate trainees whose work
skills are not developed. In some cases, they are willing to hire
trainees with very poor skills and are even willing to absorb the
costs of teaching the youngster the work, virtually from scratch.
But the items which seem to cause employers the most trouble
when they hire Mobilization's youngsters are lateness and poor
attendance.

> The problem with your kids is their lousy attitude toward the
> work. Your training is not sufficient to allow them to keep pace with
> the rest of the people here but I don't care much about that . . .
> we can teach them ourselves. But, when they come in late, smoke,
> drink, and socialize while at their machines? I can't have too much
> of that, it gets out of hand after a while.

A survey of 530 trainees in 1966 who were hired and started to
work, showed that 23 percent were either dismissed by their employers or quit on their own. (It should be noted that this figure is
not markedly different from the turnover rates of the general population between seventeen and nineteen years of age.) Of the factors cited by employers in terminating Mobilization's trainees, almost 60 percent gave as either the prime or the contributing reason
the fact that the trainees were absent from work too many times
or were continually late.

TABLE III. REASONS FOR DISMISSAL OF MFY TRAINEES

N = 117

Continued lateness and/or absence from work	58
Inattentive or disinterested in his work	20
Could not meet the education or skill requirements of the job	16

Insubordination	9
Theft or illegal acts	5
Poor appearance	1
Other reasons (medical, lack of work, drafted into service)	8

The personnel director of a large department store places the blame for this on Mobilization in that "these kids were not oriented to what job requirements really are—such as, a five-day week doesn't mean three days and that their coming in at 10:00 A.M. when the job starts at 9:00 A.M. is not up to them."

> W. C. seemed interested in the work; he learned what he had to learn and was accepted by all of us. We understood his circumstances, and we really hoped he would work out his problems. His attendance was so erratic that I felt I would do neither of us a favor by keeping him on the job. He had no time responsibility. We weren't upset over five or fifteen minutes, but when it was a matter of three or four hours, several times a week, we had no choice but to let him go.
> I wanted to help him, but I didn't know it would be that painful. If he didn't show up when he was supposed to, the work just didn't get done, and I ended up doing a day and a half's work.

In a very few cases an employer will put up with a trainee's poor attendance. There is no pattern evident here except that, when an employer is satisfied with the work that the trainee produces, he may be more inclined to overlook a sloppy attendance record. "Sure he's late: It is not unusual—lateness is common with everybody, and these kids are no different. I've never had workers who were too accurate when it came to the time they should come to work." This employer was willing to put up with erratic attendance because the boys were good workers "once they got started." In many other cases, especially where the trainee has not worked out to the firm's expectation, the problem of poor attendance and continued lateness is often the last straw.

Special Incentives to Hiring

Employers are willing to hire trainees supplied by a program such as Mobilization for several reasons, ranging from a sense of obligation to more specific incentives. Employers may be attracted to the agency because it offers them a steady, dependable supply of relatively cheap and disposable labor. Marginal firms depend on a readily available pool of cheap labor to maintain themselves in business. Many of these firms are characterized by a very low level of capital utilization—that is, they use a lot of labor with little machinery—and it is vital for them to keep their wage bill as low as possible. It is not unusual in these cases to find a firm's labor force made up of a large percentage of young minority-group workers. The use of such labor not only helps to keep a firm alive, but also provides a useful work experience for young entrants to the labor market—a work experience which is not sheltered and which represents real work in real work situations.

Although most trainees are hired at the minimum wage, it is possible for an employer to effect some small savings in his wage bill through the use of an on-the-job-training contract, an agreement under which the agency reimburses the employer a set sum for employing and training the agency's client for a stipulated time period. This reimbursement may constitute up to 40 percent of the employer's wage bill. The owner of a woodworking plant, for example, says that using Mobilization trainees has worked out very well for him. He said he would not keep most of the boys under different circumstances, but since he is paying only 60 percent of their salary, he is more patient.

Mobilization's job-development staff underwrites the on-the-job-training contracts and makes regular field visits to check on both the trainee and the employer. The intention is to keep tabs on the client's progress and to make certain that the employer is not abusing the terms of the contract. Employers tend to live up to the terms of the agreement, and many trainees have been hired as regular employees at the end of their on-the-job-training. Often, however, the employer has sufficient cause for letting the trainee go at the termination of the contract, and this is not disputed. The most effective way of "selling" a trainee to a prospective employer is through the on-the-job-training contract. It limits the employer's risk and, at the same time, allows the trainee to make errors and learn from them without penalizing his trainer.

The successful use of on-the-job-training contracts has depended in large measure on the size of the firm involved. Large firms—banks, insurance companies, and industrial corporations—are often unwilling to bother with the red tape that accompanies the contract. For many of them, the slight saving on their wage bill is of less consequence than the additional paperwork. Small firms, on the other hand, will often hire a trainee only if a contract can be written for the job. The extent to which the on-the-job-training contract has been used by Mobilization depends in part on the availability of the Federal funds which underwrite the agency's share of the costs. When the funds have been available, the job-development section has been able to write almost four hundred contracts in a year.[2]

Conclusions

In most cases, Mobilization has taken great care to ensure that prospective employers know what the agency is all about, and how trainees are likely to perform. When an employer hires a Mobilization trainee, he generally does not expect a finished worker, and the graduates of Mobilization's training program usually are not terminated from their jobs because of any gross lack of skills. Employers want kids who will show up for work when they are supposed to, who can be counted on to come back after lunch, and who will call in if they are sick. In short, they are willing to accept youngsters with rudimentary skills, but they insist on decent work habits and attitudes. Mobilization's training program is designed to teach just these work attitudes, but the fact that over 70 percent of trainee terminations can be traced to poor habits and attitudes is a clear indication that better training methods need to be devised. In addition, greater emphasis must be placed on teaching the trainee how to learn once he gets on a job.

To deal more adequately with problems of motivation and atti-

2 For further discussing of on-the-job training see the paper "Advanced and Posttraining Programs" in this volume.

tude, the agency experimented with group counseling methods. These seemed promising but were not used as an integral part of the program since this would have interfered with the research design. The case of Benjamin is instructive.

> Benjamin was a very passive participant in the group. He was reluctant to express himself in English, even though he had come from Puerto Rico three years earlier. He understood the discussions but participated only marginally. It was only after he was sent on a referral for a messenger-boy job and was rejected by the employer that he was able to speak animatedly in the group. With some hesitation, he began to talk about his interview and reported that he was rejected because of his "poor English." When another member of the group pointed out that Benjamin was speaking to the group in English with no difficulty, it became evident that this was a job that Benjamin was not interested in and really did not want to do. He had presented himself to the employer in such a way that he was rejected. Benjamin began to relate more freely to the group, since the others now knew that he could do so. He was subsequently placed as a solderer in a large manufacturing firm, having successfully completed a job application and gone through an employment interview.[3]

It must be emphasized that the problem of job success for every trainee cannot be solved simply by persuading employers to set realistic entrance and testing standards or by dealing with a trainee's motivational and attitudinal problems. Ultimately the economy must produce a sufficient number of jobs, either in the private sector or in some sort of public-works program.[4] The best motiva-

[3] Abraham Helfand, "Group Counseling as an Approach to the Work Problems of Disadvantaged Youth," *Rehabilitation Counseling Bulletin,* Vol. 11 (December 1967), p. 113.

[4] Since only a small percentage of the nation's youth are enrolled in work-training programs, the placement of trainees is not, in and of itself, a solution to youth employment. "The growing problem in all this is . . . whether or not the economy is really going to be able to absorb these youngsters as well as a lot of other children who are either moderately capable or very capable. . . . What you probably need is a public works program. Planning for this should go on now." Melvin Herman and Stanley Sadofsky, *Youth Work Programs* (New York, Graduate School of Social Work, New York University, 1966), p. 37.

tion for training is a guaranteed job that one wants. This motivates not only the trainee but also the potential employer; if he needs workers, he can be expected to make efforts to see that trainees learn their jobs. Many observers have noted that during World War II, many people who were previously not qualified for jobs were effectively and quickly trained to do them.

A work-training program like Mobilization's must continually work with employers so that testing and job classifications do not act as a bar to trainee placement. At the same time, it must agitate for the development of a sufficient number of meaningful and useful jobs.[5] It also is likely that job development and placement are best made the function of a separate unit, as at Mobilization, since they are the core around which other parts of an employment program must rotate.

[5] For a discussion of this point see David Wellman, "The Wrong Way to Find Jobs for Negroes," *Transaction* (April, 1968), pp. 9–18.

9

An Appraisal of Youth Employment Programs

Harold H. Weissman

People who are interested in Mobilization often ask, "Are you successful with the teen-agers in your training program?" Essentially, their criterion of success is the number of teen-agers placed in employment. This view of training programs may be eminently reasonable from the point of view of a public-spirited citizen, but no easy answer can be given to the question.

Merely placing a trainee on a job is seldom a sign of success. Does he remain on the job for any period of time? Is there any chance for advancement? Can placing him in a job for which there is only seasonal need be regarded as success?

At Mobilization, the underlying principle has been that out-of-school, hard-to-employ young people can find and hold a place in the job world if they are given suitable training. This suggests that training makes a difference. It follows from this position that a trainee should be able to hold a job after completing his training and that, as a result of both training and experience at Mobilization, he should be able to maintain himself in the job market.[1]

[1] As noted in the chapter titled "Overview of Employment Opportunities" in this volume, the research project, "An Experiment to Test Three Major Issues of Work Program Methodology" carried out in conjunction with the Columbia University School of Social Work Research Center, should provide significant data upon which to make a judgment of this contention. The results of this study are expected to be available in late 1969.

TABLE I. WORK-CREW OUTCOME RECORD
July 1, 1964–May 30, 1965

N = 431

	Number	Percentage
Positive Outcome	209	49
Employed; returned to school; placed in training (sent to trade school, on-the-job training, or private employment)		
Neutral Outcome	148	34
Left area; left MFY because of family or medical problems; in counseling at MFY (may be unemployed but still keeps counselor contact)		
Negative Outcome	74	17
Unemployed; arrested; lost contact		

The outcome figures given in Table I for a typical period on the one hand show a great deal more success than failure. On the other hand, they give rise to some doubts concerning the meaning of the positive-outcome category. It is unlikely that more than 25 percent of the total group got jobs that promised job security and an opportunity for advancement.[2] Probably another 25 to 30 percent had increased employability as a result of participation, but this is an extremely difficult concept to measure.

> Employability is a lot of things. It's partly the self-image of the kid; it's partly the image he is able to project to the employer; it's partly what skills he's got or can gain; and it's partly a question of how much education he has. . . . There is considerable difficulty in specifying an appropriate yardstick for such . . . items as literacy and attitude toward work, in weighing these resources, and in combining them properly.[3]

[2] The research project will trace the employment history of MFY trainees for several years after their completion of the program, by monitoring their social-security payments. This phase of the study will not be completed until 1970.

[3] Melvin Herman and Stanley Sadofsky, *Youth Work Programs* (New York, New York University Graduate School of Social Work, 1966), p. 39.

In addition to the problem of specifying indexes of success, a number of other factors must be considered in evaluating the outcomes of the program: (1) The client population includes the most deprived segment of youth in the country, socially, culturally, and intellectually. (2) The availability of jobs, over which MFY has little or no control, accounts for a considerable portion of failure. (3) Many trainees who drop out of the program have found jobs on their own, and many others eventually return to the program. (4) Finally, placement on a job, in itself, is a poor criterion for vocational success—there are few teen-agers, rich, poor, or otherwise, who do not have several jobs before settling into one.

Notwithstanding the problems of measurement, MFY has certain basic goals which are regarded as the minimum essential for success. The trainee should have at least one set of marketable skills; he should be aware of what employers expect in the way of work attitudes and habits; he should know how to use employment counseling and other services of social agencies once he leaves Mobilization, especially those designed for occupational upgrading.

A great deal has been learned about achieving these goals. Cloward and Ontell have suggested that the major problem that youth-employment programs must address is the trainees' sense of competence.

> Despite all that is said about disadvantaged youth today, they do not seem any more deprived than the children of poor families throughout our history. In absolute terms, as a matter of fact, they are better off. . . . What is different . . . is the context in which they find themselves, for that context makes them relatively worse off. The chief contextual change is in the occupational world. Skills required to obtain and hold employment have shifted and will doubtless shift much more. . . . What contemporary slum and minority youth probably lack that similar children in earlier periods possessed is not motivation but some minimal sense of competence. . . . One's sense of competence results from an appraisal of self in relation to some context. A young person who has no feeling that he can master the jobs available in the modern world is not likely to exhibit many of the psychological and social traits the absence of which we mistakenly call "poor motivation." [4]

[4] Richard A. Cloward and Robert Ontell, "Our Illusions About Training," *American Child*, (January 1965), pp. 6–7.

The Mobilization experience clearly bears out the implication that the emphasis in youth-employment programs should not blur the problems that exist in the social structure. The best kind of training in the world will not suffice if the economy does not produce enough jobs and if schools are not providing the skills necessary to master the jobs. Setting up training programs should not divert us from seeing to it that jobs are made available and that schools educate their students.

Until the schools and the economy work more effectively, youth-employment programs will be needed. In designing programs to produce competent graduates, a number of ideas can be derived from Mobilization's experience. It is clear, for example, that from 10 to 15 percent of the applicants at Mobilization had severe emotional handicaps which limited their employment possibilities: drug addiction, various forms of psychosis, and mental retardation, as well as physical disabilities. Some form of sheltered-workshop program is required for this group.

The poorest results were achieved with the sixteen- and seventeen-year-old trainees.[5] They were, as a group, immature, not particularly concerned with planning for the future, and prone to quit jobs for frivolous reasons. In addition, the presence of large numbers of young teen-agers had the effect of keeping more mature teen-agers away from the program. Some form of special program akin to the work-orientation program would seem appropriate for the younger trainees. Another approach to the problem of the younger trainee would be to develop a new form of vocational high school. Clearly there is a need for change in vocational and general secondary-school education in the slum. Instead of designing youth-employment programs for sixteen- and seventeen-year-olds, it might be wiser to redesign the vocational high school. These schools are not adequately educating youth for employment

---

[5] The Civilian Conservation Corps (CCC) of the depression years was not taken as a model for youth-employment programs in the 1960's primarily because trainees in the CCC did not really learn trades usable once they returned to civilian life. Yet the high visibility of CCC projects—building parks, recreation areas, etc.—and the attendant prestige of being a part of such projects may have added to CCC trainees' morale and motivation. The Neighborhood Youth Corps does not offer many such opportunities for public recognition.

and are producing dropouts. Vocational education in high schools is now geared to the crafts and trades, and these industries are not expanding. One thing that is needed is an increase in training in the vocational high schools for the one area that *is* expanding—the service area.

For older teen-agers and young adults, MFY's experience has helped to clarify a number of issues in the youth employment field. Emphasis should be placed on imparting job skills in work areas where there is a possibility of gaining employment. Attitudes and work habits are best taught in this context. Skill training has to be carried on in an organized and programmed manner. For dropouts, who make up the majority of Mobilization's trainee population, remedial education is most readily accepted when it is tied in to skill training.

Trainees clearly lack knowledge about the employment world.[6] Employment programs must make up this deficit. Group discussions and counseling can be useful methods of dealing with this problem. Peer support can also be an important source of assistance to trainees. At one time the idea of a trainee union was considered, but it was eventually dropped. Such a union, oriented not only toward the training program but also toward outside employment, might have a number of beneficial effects in breaking down barriers to employment, advising members of employment opportunities, and interpreting the training program to employers and adults. In addition, a union might follow up on trainees who have left the program but are having difficulty finding work.

The initial image that an employment program presents to trainees is of crucial significance. Mobilization was able to halve its preprogram dropout rate by instituting a variety of procedures to bring the potential trainee into training as quickly as possible—help in getting working papers, a bilingual staff, immediate follow-up on broken appointments, health and medical assistance, etc. A promising innovation was the development of a vocational-evaluation

---

[6] This is also, surprisingly, an area in which many vocational counselors are deficient. Although they know about basic requirements for jobs, they are less knowledgeable about market conditions, whether basic job requirements are realistic, and the conditions under which employers can be induced to open up job opportunities. See the chapter on "The Problem of Job Placement" in this volume for amplification.

unit to assist trainees in understanding the range of occupational choices they might have. The fact that Mobilization offered a wide variety of employment programs considerably increased its effectiveness: dispersed work, work crews, trade training, on-the-job-training, direct placement. Each of these programs had particular advantages for particular types of trainees.[7]

Conclusions

In late 1966, Mobilization For Youth, in recognition of its efforts, was designated by the Federal government as one of eight national Manpower Research Training Laboratories. However one evaluates the success of Mobilization's work-training programs, they are a clear statement to the general public that low-income youths need help in finding employment. The affluent youngster is allowed to postpone employment commitment almost to the age of thirty. He is likely to have a family to fall back on, friends who can assist him, and some access to money—three important sources of support. MFY's work-training programs attempted to provide low-income youths with counterparts to these advantages. A program is seldom as good as a family, but it is almost a necessity when there is no family.

However, the problem of youth unemployment cannot be solved apart from the general problem of employment in the economy. No amount of training will suffice if there is no need for workers. From this vantage point it is clear that the soundest economic policy is to keep youth in school—first, because there is no shortage of unskilled labor; second, because the economy now requires more education for occupational success.[8] Thus, while employment programs are required for dropouts and for those who need additional training after high school, the major emphasis should be

[7] The idea has been advanced by some that training programs should be offered as they were offered to veterans under the G.I. Bill. This would ensure a wide variety of programs and the opportunity to choose.

[8] Lynton argues that one of the main advantages of keeping low-income youths in school is that the high-school diploma serves as an index to employeers of social acceptability—that the potential employee is not a "problem." Edith Lynton, "Will They Be Hired?" *American Child*, (January 1965), p. 13.

placed on revamping the secondary educational system, both the vocational and general, for low-income youth.

Over ten thousand applicants came to Mobilization during its first five years of operation. Considering the rather small geographical area from which applicants were accepted, this suggests that the problem of youth employment is of immense magnitude. It is hoped that the policies and programs suggested in these papers will help to ease this problem and support the hopes and aspirations of the countless youngsters who wait to be served.

PART II

Educational Opportunities

10

Overview of Educational Opportunities

Harold H. Weissman

In the year 1848, Edward Sheldon, later superintendent of schools for the city of Oswego, New York, established a school for "rude and untrained Irish boys and girls between the ages of five and twenty-one." As Sheldon expressed his conception of education, "the object is not so much to impart information as to educate the senses; arouse, quicken, and develop the perceptive faculties; teach children to observe; and awaken the sense of inquiry." [1]

Periodic attempts were made later in the nineteenth and twentieth centuries to improve the quality of American education. Some of these attempts were specifically geared to minority groups—the American Indian, Negro freedmen before and after the Civil War, the slum children in the large metropolitan areas around the turn of the century. In 1956 the current phase of educational reform began, spurred by the sudden realization that American education could no longer be assumed to be in the forefront. The post-Sputnik period also brought increased awareness that the children of low-income minorities were not being adequately educated. The 1954 Supreme Court desegregation decree had already alerted the country to the educational problems of the Negro minority.

During the planning period for Mobilization, the educational problems uncovered in the area were immense. In 1962 there were sixteen elementary schools and five junior high schools. The ele-

[1] Edward A. Sheldon, *Course of Study,* Oswego Schools, 1859–60, as quoted in Garda Bowman and Gordon Klopf, *Teacher Education in a Social Context* (New York, Banks Street School of Education, 1966).

119

mentary schools had a total enrollment of 15,706 pupils, approximately 12,500 of whom lived in the Mobilization area. The junior
high schools had an enrollment of 7,555, an estimated 3,800 of
whom were Mobilization-area residents. There were in addition
two high schools—a vocational high school which drew its student
population from the city as a whole, and an academic high school
with 2,800 pupils, which served the southeast portion of Manhattan. Dropout rates for grades nine through twelve were 9.9 percent
for the total city but 11.8 percent in the Mobilization area.[2]
Within the area 78.6 percent of the dropouts from grade seven to
twelve were one to six years retarded in reading. A third of the
adult population had an eighth-grade education or less. A particular problem for the Lower East Side schools was the large and increasing numbers of children who came from homes where little
or no English was spoken.

Mobilization undertook to deal with this situation by setting up
education programs in five basic categories: (1) teacher training,
(2) curriculum improvement, (3) parent-community relations,
(4) reading and other learning problems of pupils, and (5) guidance and attendance services. The overall goal of these programs
—the goal of all educational efforts in slum areas—was stated by
Cloward and Jones as follows:

> Equality means that the educational system shall not be organ-
> ized in such a way as to favor children who are socialized in one
> rather than another part of the social structure. Differentials in
> socialization, arising from socio-economic position and ethnic ori-
> gin, must, like individual differences in learning, also be adjusted to
> by the school system. If the educational enterprise is simply an ex-
> tension of the middle-class home, then it follows that only middle-
> class children will tend to do well in it. If the school fails to prac-
> tice equality in these several respects, then it can be understood as
> contributing to the very problem which it otherwise deplores.[3]

[2] Tamara Obrebska, "School Dropouts, (mimeographed, New York, Mobilization For Youth, 1963).
[3] Richard A. Cloward and James A. Jones, "Social Class: Educational
Attitudes and Participation" (mimeographed, New York, Columbia University School of Social Work, July 1962), p. 3. "Our system of education
places a strong stress upon doing rather than being, upon a future orienta-

Teacher Training

As is true of most slums, teachers in the MFY area generally lived elsewhere. Most of them were unfamiliar with lower-class life styles.[4] A study of the career pattern of Chicago public-school teachers indicates that teachers typically begin their careers in lower-class neighborhoods, where there are more vacancies, and transfer out as soon as they can.[5] Thus the teachers with the least experience are found most often in low-income areas. This fact, in addition to the personal and learning problems of the children, means that the time spent on discipline or organizational details often ranges between 50 percent and 80 percent of the school day,[6] leaving relatively little time for actual instruction. Teachers in slum schools, then, need special help to upgrade their skills, and particularly to alert them to the needs and techniques of dealing with youngsters whose backgrounds and experience are generally far different from those of the teacher.

The Mobilization Proposal sketched out three programs in teacher training. Teachers from six elementary schools were to participate in a School-Community Relations Program, an intensive in-service course in community relations which would include visiting the homes of pupils. In a proposed program of Laboratory Schools, one elementary school and one junior high were to be

---

tion rather than an orientation toward the present or the past, upon the notion that man is superordinate to nature rather than in harmony with it or subjugated by it, upon the notion that man is flexible and plastic and capable of change rather than that he is essentially, and perhaps immutably, evil. A child who has not acquired these particular value orientations in his home and community is not so likely to compete successfully with youngsters among whom these values are implicitly taken for granted. Part of the problem of underachievement among some lower-class persons may therefore be attributed to the existence of these alternative value orientations to which the young are differentially socialized." *Ibid.*

[4] Generally teachers are born into the lower middle class and acquire full middle-class status through professional education. See Donald E. Super, *The Psychology of Careers* (New York, Harper and Bros., 1957), p. 244.

[5] Howard Becker, "The Career of a Chicago Public School Teacher," *American Sociological Review,* Vol. 17, No. 7 (July 1952), pp. 470–76.

[6] Martin T. Deutsch, *Minority Group and Class Status as Related to Social and Personality Factors in Scholastic Achievements,* (mimeograph No. 2 (New York: The Society for Applied Anthropology, 1960), p. 23.

selected in the local area in which innovative programs would be developed. Student teachers recruited from teachers' colleges were to be assigned to these schools for training. The object of the program was to raise the status of teaching in low-income neighborhoods by giving young teachers a sense of the challenge involved in this work. It was hoped that the program would help to overcome the tendency of teachers to regard the slum schools as merely an unpleasant preliminary to employment in suburban or middle-income schools.[7]

The third program, Training for Improved Language-Arts Instruction, was to include in-service courses carrying graduate credit and offered on an extension basis: a course on the early identification and correction of reading difficulties; and a course focused on techniques of language instruction for non-English-speaking pupils.

Curriculum Improvement

In the field of curriculum improvement, Mobilization's central proposal was the creation of a Curriculum Planning Committee and a curriculum materials center. The curriculum center would develop materials specifically geared for minority groups. The committee would work on setting up displays of the center's work, disseminate the material for the use of teachers, and publish a bulletin for teachers concerning the facilities and services of the center. In addition, special curriculum coordinators were to be appointed for twelve of the elementary schools, to assist teachers through observations, conferences, and help in the location and use of new curriculum materials, particularly those developed by the center.

Parent-Community Programs

Contrary to the belief of many people, low-income parents generally attach a high value to education.[8] Most parents interviewed by Mobilization recognized the need for education in order to get

[7] The Laboratory School never became fully operational, as authority could seldom be secured from the Board of Education to try out innovative programs. The long delays in negotiating with the board ultimately made the concept unworkable.

[8] For discussion of these issues, see Cloward and Jones, *op. cit.*

ahead. Yet they did not always translate this attitude into active assistance and cooperation with the schools in furthering their children's education. Mobilization's Parent Education Program was designed to promote this active involvement. A core of local residents were to be trained to visit parents at home, discuss problems with them, encourage friendly parent-teacher relations, and organize informal discussion groups devoted to matters of common interest.

Reading and Learning Problems

The Mobilization Proposal offered a number of programs designed to improve reading instruction. Reading centers were to be established in each of the elementary schools in the area, equipped with a variety of materials for the improvement of reading skills, including teaching machines. Reading clinics to provide diagnostic and remedial services were proposed for two elementary schools. In addition, the Mobilization Proposal discussed a number of programs to help the very young with the transition from home to school. The Early Childhood and Enrichment Project was to provide experimental classes to improve the school readiness of four- and five-year-olds and the school adjustment of first graders. The Ungraded Primary Program was to experiment with instruction at two elementary schools in which the kindergarten or first through the third year would be treated as a unit, with no grade divisions. Finally, the Homework Helper Program was to test whether high-school sophomores and juniors of low-income families could be employed successfully after school as tutors to elementary-school pupils.

Guidance and Attendance

In the matter of guidance, the accepted New York State standard is three hundred pupils to one counselor, but the ratio of New York City high schools as of 1961 was 641 to one; in the junior high schools, it was 1,710 to one.[9] MFY proposed to place a full-time guidance counselor in every elementary school in the area

[9] Rose Shapiro, "Report of the Mayor's Conference on Labor, Industry and Employment," (New York, New York City Youth Board, 1961), p. 25.

which did not currently have one. The number of attendance teachers was also to be increased so there would be one for every junior high school in the area. In addition, a Small Groups Program was to be instituted under the guidance of social group workers with clinical experience, designed to improve the classroom behavior and school achievement of emotionally disturbed children through group therapy.[10]

Scope of the Program

Mobilization's intent was to act as an instrument of change and innovation in the public-school system. Its overall success in achieving this aim is discussed in the last paper in this volume. During the first five years of its existence many issues were faced: whether the program should be devoted to developing new techniques or merely to providing the personnel and money to expand the use of older techniques; whether all the schools on the Lower East Side should be served or whether the resources should be concentrated in one or two schools; whether professional teachers should determine the policies and practices of the schools or whether these should be in the hands of the citizens. In the course of facing these issues, a severe rupture in relations between the schools and MFY occurred. In addition, many of the original programs were altered, some were abandoned without ever being tried, and new ones were developed. These crises, program shifts, and changes are discussed in the papers that follow.[11]

[10] A program designed in part from the knowledge gained in the Small Groups Program is described in detail in the chapter on "New Programs for Group Work Agencies" in Vol. 1, *Individual and Group Services.*

[11] Budgets for the Education Division were as follows: 1962–63, $576,-000,00; 1963–64, $1,254,628.00; 1964–65, $1,225,965.00; 1965–66, $1,230,-714.00; 1966–67 $844,738.00. These figures do not include indirect costs for fiscal services, executive offices, public information, central services, personnel department, and occupancy costs. Indirect costs averaged 25 percent per year. In contrast to other MFY divisions, many staff members of the Education Division, in order to retain their status and benefits as Board of Education personnel, were merely attached to MFY. Their paychecks were issued through the Board of Education, even though Mobilization provided the funds. Problems related to this funding procedure are discussed in the concluding paper in this section. The City of New York provided the funds for the Board of Education personnel attached to Mobilization. The Ford Foundation provided funds for the programs carried out by non-Board of Education personnel.

11

Parent Education Program

Henry Heifetz

The Parent Education Program was originally projected as a way of establishing contact with newly arrived families in the neighborhood, in-migrants who, it was presumed, were still arriving in considerable numbers from Puerto Rico. In 1962, the program was part of the Division of Educational Opportunities, and contacts with in-migrants were made through the schools.

The Engagement with the Schools

Once the general program coordinator had been selected, the selection of the Parent Education aides was undertaken. The aides were to be community people "with an ability to establish relationships with adults." Eight workers were finally selected for assignment to all junior high schools in the MFY area; later two elementary schools were included. Among those chosen as aides were three who spoke Spanish as well as English and one part-time worker who was fluent in Chinese. For about the first six months, the aides received on-the-job training. First, working as a team and then assigned to separate schools, working directly with the school administration, they began the process of visiting homes.

The families initially chosen for visits were those of children listed in the school records of new admissions, on the assumption that a large proportion of these families would be new arrivals to the neighborhood. The aides were instructed to explore and encourage the interest of the parents in the school and to attempt to

125

form them into small groups. The list of objectives of the program distributed to the administration of the participating schools as well as to the aides, included the following:

1. To identify the newcomers and take steps to make the family feel welcome.
2. To give information about community resources.
3. To create a climate in which newcomers can share their fears and confusion about the newness of the area and their home and community problems.
4. To develop a beginning sense of identity with the community by locating some familiar institutions, neighbors, shops, etc.
5. To explore the school experiences of their children that might be bothersome to either parents or children.
6. To prepare for possible solutions to school conflicts by acknowledging the problem and suggesting sources of help.
7. To increase the school's responsiveness to lower-class life styles by interpreting obstacles that new families of that class experience in their contact with the school.
8. To improve parents' potential as role models for their children by giving them a clear image of what happens in school and by stimulating curiosity about and broadening their knowledge of community life.

The attempt at the outset was clearly to work within the framework of the schools. When making their visits, the parent-education aides introduced themselves as coming from the respective schools to which they were assigned and in which they had offices. They did not present themselves as MFY workers.

It was soon discovered that a considerable in-migrant population did not in fact exist on the Lower East Side. It had been assumed that a number of families were arriving on the Lower East Side (primarily from Puerto Rico) for whom the United States was an entirely new and frightening place. Actually such fresh arrivals tended to settle in East Harlem; most of the Puerto Rican children listed as new arrivals in the various schools of the Lower East Side proved to be transfers from some other school in the area or elsewhere in the city. The original emphasis of the

Parent Education Program on "introduction to the new" was largely inapplicable. As result, the aides, once they had won the confidence of the families they approached, found themselves heavily involved in more conventional kinds of service: aiding people in their relationship to authority—e.g., the courts, the Department of Welfare—health problems, housing difficulties, etc. A considerable part of their time, from the beginning, was taken up with this generalized social work.

The fact that the aides were community people and nonprofessionals immensely facilitated their contacts with the community but, in certain cases, led to an attitude of muted hostility on the part of principals, assistant principals, or guidance counselors in the schools. Even when cooperative, the school administrations tended to distrust the parent-education aides' effort to create independent organizations of parents.[1] As indicated in the statement of objectives, the Parent Education Program was meant to consider the problems of the children in school and to increase the parents' interest in the school; but just as important, the approach through the schools was meant to lead the parents into a concern with broader problems of community interest and action.

From the beginning, the Parent Education Program made an effort to remain both inside and outside the schools. The aides were instructed to interest the parents in the parent associations of the various schools, to work with these associations and explore their possibilities. At the same time, the mothers approached by the aides were organized in groups separate from the parent associations and, when attending parent-association meetings, sometimes seemed to function, in the eyes of the school administration, as intrusive pressure groups. And, of course, MFY planners meant them ultimately to be pressure groups, pushing for serious improvements in the schools. Even the more sympathetic administrators thought of the program primarily as a means of drawing more parents to the schools where they could be informed about school policies.

The existing parent associations were found to be almost totally

---

[1] Institutions like schools tend to maximize their control and discretion over such organizations as alumni groups, parents' associations, etc. The Parent Education Program threatened such control and discretion.

under the control of the school principals. The officers of these associations tended to be middle-class women in actuality or in aspiration, amenable to the guidance of the school administration. Although a number of the principals felt that the parent-education aides were useful in increasing contact with the community, most were chary of the threat to their own parent association. The groups organized by the parent-education aides were not allowed to meet in the schools, and held their meetings on various MFY premises or in private homes. The aides were continually urged by principals to bring the mothers into the parent associations because "that was the place to work for improvement."

As for tangible results during this period in the schools, the parent-education aides did succeed in organizing a certain number of groups and in making their personal presence felt in the schools. The aides were utilized in some schools for work with "difficult families." In one school, the guidance teacher followed a regular practice of referring such cases to the aide. Other aides began by concentrating on in-migrant families but, once the in-migrant population was seen to be a small one, soon expanded their activities to people with problems. Parents were involved in various community activities then being put into motion through MFY impetus, such as developing a narcotics information center and a housing clinic.

In some individual cases the parent-education aides were of great service as advocates of the rights of the children and the families in issues of possible suspension or in dealing with other school difficulties. Recreational activities were sometimes organized, such as outings, to aid in the formation of more cohesive groups. Once organized, these groups found some natural leaders among their membership but remained heavily dependent on the organizer, the parent-education aide herself, for their functioning and even their existence. They were not able to develop autonomous structures, with working executive boards. This seems also in part to have been a result of the fundamental imprecision in the program: Was it to work within the school and therefore be limited by school authorities, or outside the school and be free to evaluate and suggest changes? It was assumed that the groups would eventually be brought into the schools, not to become absorbed in the parent associations but to operate in their own right and under their own power. The method and structure by which this was to be achieved were left undefined.

In September 1963 the Parent Education Program was shifted from the Education Division to the Community Development Division. Two reasons were given for the change. One was that the program belonged by its nature more in Community Development than in the more highly technical education program. Two—and perhaps the most cogent reason—was because the program would have greater freedom of operation in this division.

The fact that an in-migrant education program was not a vital necessity on the Lower East Side no doubt contributed to the decision. There was also some question as to whether it might be preferable to work with the elementary schools rather than the junior high schools which were the initial target of the program, in order to get to educational and familial problems at an earlier stage of their development. Most important, difficulties were increasing with the school administrations. These difficulties reached their crisis in the Mobilization Of Mothers incident, as a result of which the parent-education aides left the schools.

MOM and Its Aftermath

We the school principals of districts 1, 2, 3, 4 Manhattan hereby demand an investigation of Mobilization For Youth and ask for the removal of Mr. George Brager, its director of action programs, whose activities with parent education and community organization workers has resulted in these workers becoming full-time paid agitators and organizers for extremist groups. This constitutes an abuse of the noble purpose for which great sums of Federal and municipal money were originally appropriated. This movement has been subverted from its original plan to war against delinquency into a war against individual schools and their leaders, to what purpose we cannot at the present time divine. These groups have attacked principals and the schools in an irrational and irresponsible manner. They have created a situation which is demoralizing and undermining the sincere and dedicated efforts of our professional leaders who voluntarily render their services in this difficult but challenging area of the city. While they have on the one hand met

with us principals and superintendent to resolve the various difficulties that have arisen as a result of these parent and community-
group activities, they have on the other hand continued and
broadened their untruthful attack on our work. We can and will
document all of our charges.

Principals, districts 1, 2, 3, 4 Manhattan

With this telegram, sent on January 28, 1964, to the sources
of MFY's funding (with copies to newspapers and various political
figures), the principals of the Lower East Side schools began their
attempt to protect one of their number and immobilize Mobilization. It was the preface for the full-scale attack on Mobilization
later launched in the pages of the New York *Daily News*. The telegram was sent because a small group of mothers was attempting
to force removal of a principal who, in their opinion, had shown
himself to be arrogant, dictatorial, and contemptuous in his opinions and treatment of lower-class mothers and children. In sub-
urbia, such an accusation leads to removal or, at the very least,
apology and explanation. Money and influence are rarely insulted
by bureaucrats concerned with retirement pay and promotion.[2] On
the Lower East Side, however, even principals who were satisfied
with the Parent Education Program and later indicated some willingness to continue using parent-education personnel, in this case,
joined ranks to protect their structure, their values, their futures.

Mobilization of Mothers (MOM) was a small community group
which had organized outside the Parent Education Program. Responsibility for the program was shifted to the parent-education
corodinator (who had already been put under the Community Organizing section of the Community Development Division) when
concern with the administration of P.S. 140 had become the focus
of Mobilization Of Mothers' activities. When the telegram quoted
above was sent, MOM had been under the supervision of the
Parent Education Program for only a couple of months, but previous irritations with MFY's "meddling" in the schools made the

[2] In low-income areas there is a class-structured expectation on the part of
most school administrators that parents do not have the ability to evaluate
the schools and therefore that the school officials know best. The results are
paternalism and the denial of the right of parents collectively to seek
changes in the school.

MOM incident seem "the last straw," precipitating the principals' actions.[3]

The MOM incident is more fully documented in other papers.[4] What is important for the Parent Education Program is that the controversy dragged on for a couple of months until the position of the aides in the schools had finally become untenable, and the aides were taken out of the schools. The groups that had been formed dissolved, although a few members provided the nucleus for later groups formed outside the schools. A participant in the decisions at that time gives the following summary.

> The workers were so intimidated that they were happy really to try to organize groups outside the school system. During this time it should be said that we continued a slow and unfruitful practice of negotiating with the top personnel in the district, including principals and the acting assistant superintendent, to try to get on a different footing in the public schools, on the theory that the easiest way to organize persons around school issues was to use the school as a base. By November of 1964 we were essentially out of the school system, though for one solid school year we were meeting regularly with the principals to try to iron out the differences.

In at least one instance, a parent-education aide had established so fruitful a relationship with the administration of a particular school that they were eager for her to continue working with them despite the general removal of the aides. This was not possible, however, because no overall agreement could be worked out between Mobilization and the school system. The Parent Education Program in the schools ended, and the aides, after a period of hesitation as to programming, were put to work on the creation of block organizations.

[3] Mobilization of Mothers was probably the first of many public disputes between school officialdom and citizens in low-income areas that occurred in New York between 1964 and 1967, when the Bundy Report urged decentralization and local control over schools.

[4] See the paper "The Attack on Mobilization" in Vol. 2, *Community Development*. See also the concluding paper in this volume.

Outside the Schools: The Block Groups

At this time in the program, late 1964, the parent-education aides were assigned the responsibility for organizing various streets, and a group of organizations was instituted—the Sixth Street Mothers, Seventh Street Mothers, Eleventh Street Mothers, etc. Some of these were vestiges of old groups, and others were newly formed. While schools remained a major concern to this community, it was a very difficult task to try to organize on a door-to-door situation with parents who had children of different ages, going to different schools. And it was very difficult to move these little groups into action, because there was no common basis for them.

Some of the groups functioned for a while, carried on a few activities, and vanished. Others, such as the 6th Street group, lasted and remained active. Those that remained relatively active did not maintain a large connection with school issues or any direct presence in the schools. The name of the program was changed to Community Education, further indicating the failure of the older program. But the supervisors of the program were still interested in getting back into the schools:

> It had long been my view that it was terribly important to get back into the school system. I did not really think that it was possible to effect any cooperative working relationship or change outside of the system. It was also my belief that if you want to organize parents as parents because their children are in school, then it follows obviously that the school is a base.

P.S. 188—the Last Attempt:

In February 1966, an experienced parent-education aide and a student worker were assigned to P.S. 188. The decision was made to base the process of organization around the individual classroom. The P.S. 188 project was an experiment; if the program proved successful, a larger-scale return to the schools was planned.

> We had agreed on certain ground rules. For example, we insisted that any class we would work with would have to have the voluntary cooperation of the teacher. . . . The idea of the class basis

was a very simple one; we simply felt that to organize around such an amorphous thing as educational issues required a common denominator. If Johnny from one family and Mary from another had Miss X as a teacher, then that's what those parents had in common.

The original intention was to start with the first grade—"when parents were still freshly attuned and interested." This proved to be impossible, because a Mobilization research project related to teaching reading, was involved with the first graders at 188. The project was therefore transferred to the second grade. It was somewhat delayed by the necessity to meet with the second-grade faculty to explain the program, as had already been done with the first-grade faculty.

The goals of the P.S. 188 project were similar to the original objectives of the Parent Education Program, but with more emphasis on the parent associations.

Our logic was of course involvement of the parents of this particular classroom in the education process of their children and in a cooperative working relationship with school personnel, and that meant the same thing that it always had, to open up two-way communication that had not previously existed with these families and persons from the school. At the first Parent Association meeting that our staff attended, out of a student body of a thousand, seven parents came. So our second and longer-range goal was to attempt through the process of involving these parents to strengthen the parent association. We conceived of it as a sort of three-headed project in the sense that the three basic elements were the parent-education aide, the school personnel (usually the principal and the teacher), and the parent association.

The parent-education aide and the student worker each visited a list of families, thirty in one case, twenty-nine in the other. Not unexpectedly, they discovered that many of the families were riddled with problems and that they could be of help:

In the first ten home visits, the parent aide discovered four families who were livid because they had recently received notices that their children were required to go to Bellevue for psychiatric examinations. The parents claimed that they had no understanding of what this was all about, so the aide had to get involved in a lengthy process with the Bureau of Child Guidance and attempt to resolve the situation. I don't think that it was fully resolved to the satisfaction of all the parents. One parent did ultimately agree that her son needed help, the other three were then put on a list for more extensive work with BCG personnel. But this is illustrative of both the alienation and the anger which the parents have for the school system.

The groups began to meet, usually in homes rather than in more public facilities. Scheduling meetings proved to be a problem in view of the many demands on the mothers. Finally each group managed to hold a meeting with the principal in which general problems were discussed, apparently with a good deal of satisfaction on both sides. It is clear that this principal was interested in genuine communication. Nevertheless, the persistence of an archaic habit of mind is illustrated by the following exchange:

> When the student worker indicated that there was certainly a strong interest on the part of these parents toward becoming engaged with the school, the principal said, "Fine; it happens that next week we are having a luncheon that the parents traditionally give the teachers. Let them come in and serve the teachers." The student, I think rather bravely, pointed out that that really was not at all what the parents had in mind and no thank you.

The president of the parent association expressed some doubt about MFY's intention, but by the end of the year the two groups were working with this parent-association in an attempt to involve the parents of all second-grade children in the school. The P.S. 188 project, in its brief life, seemed to be rather successful. There was considerable response on the part of the parents, an interested attitude in the case of the principal, and a good deal of service and organizational work by the parent education aide and the student worker. Everything seemed to point to a continuation and expansion of the program for the following school year. During the school year the MFY workers had encountered some hostility from the assistant principal and the guidance counselor, but this opposition did not seem major. Somehow or other, it, or an influence from higher up, prevailed during the summer vacation. MFY was informed that P.S. 188 did not wish to continue the project for the coming school year. Thus the last attempt to implement the objectives of the Parent Education Program within the schools had failed.

Conclusions:

The initial mistake of the Parent Education Program was its attempt to help parents adapt to the school while interesting them in changing the schools. Apparently significant change in the schools cannot be generated by internal pressure. Once the parent-education aides were in the schools, they were subject in some degree to conditions which were meant to make them useful adjuncts but not threatening critics. When the criticism became too strong, the schools fought back. The furore around Mobilization Of Mothers became a crisis point, because it was an attempt by lower-class mothers to judge the qualifications of a man who was overseeing the instruction of their children, a right which every middle-class mother takes for granted. But a break with the schools was inevitable (although it might have been gradual rather than dramatic), given the rigidity and authoritarianism of the school system.

There is considerable doubt about the value of helping parents to adapt to schools which are not interested in adapting their methods to children's educational needs.[5] Effective surveillance over a school's activities is most likely to be exercised from outside the control of the school. Those school administrators who feel themselves responsible only to their own narrow chain of command must be brought into a position of responsibility to the community of the poor. Probably this can best be accomplished through the establishment of strong organized groups concerned with education but totally independent of the schools.

[5] This is not to argue that family and environmental factors do not effect the learning ability of children, but rather to argue that schools not use the "family" factors as an excuse for not attempting change and innovation. See Robert J. Havighurst, "The Disadvantaged School," *Psychiatry and Social Science Review* (September 1968), pp. 2–5, for a discussion of all of the above factors.

12

School–Community Relations

Hettie Jones

An MFY social worker assigned to the schools faced two problem areas and was expected to deal with both of them. There was the community to be approached, studied, and, it was hoped, helped to understand the schools. And there was the school itself, to be influenced so as to make it a better vehicle for reaching and genuinely educating the community's children. In both areas of activity workers ran the risk of going counter to the policies of the host school system. Precisely because of the host-guest relationship, workers were subject to various pressures applied by the schools which could interfere with and even actively combat their work. Both the Parent Education Program and the School–Community Relations Program ran into serious difficulties of this nature.

It was hoped that the Mobilization worker in the school, equipped with a knowledge of the community and its problems frequently superior to the knowledge of the teacher or guidance counselor, would be a kind of new connecting link between the school and the ghetto community. To the schools, the worker seemed mainly a means of explaining the school to the community. The intent of the Mobilization programs, however, was to shift the weight of explanation the other way. It was mainly the school, according to MFY, that needed to improve comprehension, not the people. It was the school that should learn new ways.

The School–Community Relations Program involved a number of roles for the individual social worker, from the orthodox job of individual casework to the setting up of innovative processes for educating local teachers in the customs and values of their school and community, and finally, as in the Suspension Hearing Program, of acting as watchdog over the rights of children.

Casework Services to Schools

Under this program, social workers were assigned to selected primary and junior high schools in the MFY area. They were given office space on the premises and formally identified with the schools. Once installed, each worker developed a small case load in consultation with the school guidance counselor. A decision had been made to keep the case loads small in this program to provide an opportunity for intensive help to a limited number of problem children and their families. The cases selected were those of children with problems that were serious but not classifiably psychiatric. MFY had agreed to the Board of Education's stipulation that cases so classified were to be referred to the board's own Bureau of Child Guidance. In practice, the MFY social worker frequently handled such Bureau of Child Guidance cases, either because sufficient service could not be given by the bureau or because the child, in the midst of his problems, was still lodged on the bureau's enormous waiting list.

The average case load consisted of ten to twelve children in each school, but since the families involved were frequently large and ridden with many different problems, the worker might be directly concerned with five or six times this number of people. In a typical case, the worker would have the following contacts in one week: two sessions with the child, one session with the mother, several sessions with siblings, consultation with the guidance counselor and the teacher, and numerous contacts with other agencies—Department of Welfare, clinics, etc. The worker would deal with the concrete problems at the outset, at the same time working with the child, working with the school in interpreting the child's behavior, and educating the mother toward negotiation of the vast social system with which she was enmeshed.

The social workers in this program provided a number of services which were not new in terms of social-work aid but considerably more extensive than anything that had been offered to most of these families before. The casework methods were the traditional ones, but used here with greater flexibility than usual. To increase ease of communication, the MFY social workers tried to avoid excessive formality in the relationship between client and worker. For example, instead of having members of the family come into the worker's office, attempts were made to arrange meetings at home or in more casual community settings, such as restaurants.

A number of children in trouble and their families were helped in ways that are not subject to precise enumeration. The conditions of the work were difficult, however, and the problems of the families, while amenable to certain influences, remained interlocked and self-generative under the pressure of poverty. A caseworker in the program has described its difficulties as follows:

> It is essential to keep in mind that we were working with a captive case load. The client did not come to us voluntarily for help, and the presenting problem (child's school adjustment problem) generally revealed massive concrete and emotional problems on the part of the family. In a sense these were really the hard-core area cases, those which were unsuccessfully referred to traditional agencies, either because the client was unable to keep appointments or because the agency itself refused on the basis of what it termed the client's resistance.
>
> In addition, the problems of working in a host agency (the school) were monumental. At the outset, school people were suspicious and not understanding of the social worker's role. We were invested with a kind of magic; the feeling that by the process of referral alone, a child's behavior might change overnight. We had to underscore, again and again, that the helping process takes times and is directly connected with the child's experience both in the classroom and out. With the inception of other MFY action programs involved with the schools and parents (MOM [Mobilization Of Mothers], Parent Education, Suspense Hearings) schools grew increasingly more suspicious and hostile, which had ramifications in terms of workers' position in the school. One had the feeling that workers were tolerated in the schools and individual workers were able to "make it" on a one-to-one basis with administrators, teachers, etc., through demonstrated help to the client.
>
> The sheer physical problems of working in a host agency were difficult. The problem of space was a large one, since school rooms

were at a premium. Principals were understandably loath to give a room to a social worker who would be using the room only on a half-time basis. This problem was solved in different ways in different schools (some shared with a guidance counselor, some had a medical room, some roved the building for empty classrooms). It was generally not a satisfactory solution for either the school, the children, or the worker. The lack of a phone was quite difficult, and the constant commuting between school and agency created service gaps as well as being time- and energy-consuming for the worker. It was an expensive program from all viewpoints.

We have, I think, shown that the "unreachable" can be reached by immediate, demonstrable, concrete action. But the work is long, intensive, and arduous before client gains are made and maintained. Whether we can afford to give this long-term help (15 cases or less to a worker over a period of a year or more) is an administrative and policy issue. I wonder if we can afford not to.

The Home-Visiting Program

In line with the twofold direction of the School–Community Relations Program, toward the community and toward the school, these same social workers were also involved in a more experimental activity—the Home Visiting Program, designed to bring teachers in the schools into direct communication with all the families of their students by confronting them with the actual home situations.

This was a voluntary program for interested teachers. The program was originally conducted as a course involving earned credits and a stipend. During the first year, participating teachers attended a number of lectures by specialists on such subjects as "Family and Culture Patterns of the Community" and "Patterns of Puerto Rican Life." Visits to the homes of students were made after school hours. The incentives for participation were thus double—an opportunity for interested teachers to learn about the community, and an opportunity to make some extra money. In this first year, approximately 1,170 home visits were made by forty-five teachers.

During the second year, arrangements were made for teachers who were not interested in the lectures to visit the homes of their students, after some orientation in home visiting and interviewing techniques, and be paid separately for the time spent in visiting.

Typically, the teachers were quite anxious and fearful in anticipation of visiting in the community. However, they were pleasantly surprised at the overwhelmingly positive reception they received. Families treated them as honored guests and welcomed them into their homes. Frequently relatives or neighbors were called in to join in this festive occasion.

The social workers, in order to allay the anxiety of some of the teachers, frequently accompanied them on their first few visits. Then the worker (or the teacher herself) would suggest that a much more natural process was to go home with the child after school. It was anticipated that non-Spanish-speaking teachers would have considerable difficulty with the language barrier, but this proved to be unfounded. Generally, the Puerto Rican child served adequately enough for whatever translation was necessary.

An evaluation written in 1966 noted:

> I would say the biggest impact has been in regard to change in teacher attitude. The program has been a real eye-opener for teachers, not only in relation to seeing what low-income family life is like but also in seeing the "total child" in the classroom. It has, I think, broadened the range of what teachers view as normal behavior, while at the same time helping teachers begin to tailor their own curriculum to meet the needs of the low-income child.
>
> About one third of the teachers in this year's program have participated in previous years. These teachers return year after year, I'm convinced, because they feel the program to be helpful to them in working with the students. The money incentive, of course, cannot be minimized, but in relation to the array of after-school jobs available to teachers, it's interesting that so many choose to return to our program. . .
>
> Since the teachers are self-selected, there remains the issue of which teacher population we're reaching. It may well be that those who have come to us are already positively motivated toward MFY philosophy and stance. Thus, the hard-core bureaucratized teacher remains untouched.

One important refinement in the Home Visiting Program was elaborated during its last two years. This was the Holiday Home

Visiting Plan, in which teachers visited the homes of their children once before school started, a second time before Christmas, and a third during spring recess. Others teachers continued to visit all their students once a year on an informal basis. Both the Holiday Home Visiting group and the group carrying out more informal visits were given a certain number of orientation and spot workshops throughout the year; they also attended individual conferences with a social worker. But the Holiday Home Visiting Plan, considered an experimental group, was subjected to somewhat more structure. Teachers in this plan not only attended an orientation workshop but were given a Home Visiting Handbook (more extensive than the Home Visiting Guide given to the informal visitors) and met with a social worker in individual conferences after each visit. The families involved in this plan were themselves given an educational packet, including flash cards, suggestions to parents, a game booklet, and, for Spanish-speaking families, a Spanish-English dictionary. The results were described as follows:

The teachers have agreed overwhelmingly that the home visits, and particularly the Holiday Home Visits, have set up an effective bridge between the school and the home. Parents that would otherwise never be seen have been seen and begun to feel involved in their children's education. Open School Week visits by parents increased sharply.

One teacher in the Holiday program has been able, in the course of this year, to raise her class's reading grades (she had the bottom second grade) from preprimer to 2-2. She sees this as a two-pronged result, coming from her new attitudinal investment in the children, as well as having gotten parental involvement and follow-up through the visits.

Another teacher cites example after example in his report of the pleasure parents have felt in seeing the teacher extend himself. This feeling has been expressed not only in greater parental cooperation, but also in attitudinal changes on the part of children.

Several teachers said they began to see the child as a total person and felt they could relate better following the visits. In addition, children have used the visits as prestige symbols with peers.

A number of teachers have used this opportunity to discuss report cards at length with the families. The timing, particularly in the Holiday program, has been excellent, since the last two visits have followed on the heels of the marking periods. Several teachers have noticed improvement in academic achievement which they see as a result of these visits.

Many teachers have used the home visits as an opportunity to provide information which parents did not have, around the school itself, adult English classes, after-school activities for children, free recreational and other resources in the city. Several teachers have picked up potential family problems which they referred to the guidance counselor, before they reached the crisis stage.

Most teachers have felt that the home-visiting experience should be incorporated in some fashion in the regular school experience and in teacher-training institutions.

The Home Visiting Program succeeded to a considerable extent in easing the relations between teacher and child and between school and family. Parents, more at ease with a face and a name they knew, would often take to visiting school in other than crisis situations. Teachers came to know more about conditions on the Lower East Side than they had ever imagined was there to be known. More than a hundred teachers participated during the four years of the program, and about six thousand families were visited in their homes. With the end of MFY activities in the schools in 1966 and the transfer of the program's social workers to the neighborhood service centers, this newly constructed linkage between schools and community had to be discontinued with nothing to replace it.[1]

The Lower East Side Community Course

The Lower East Side Community Course, given through the four years of the School–Community Relations Program's existence, was intended for teachers who wanted a more academic approach toward learning about the Lower East Side. The attempt here was to lead teachers to an improvement in the quality of their

---

[1] The problems related to inducing the Board of Education to adopt successful innovations as part of the regular school programs are discussed in the paper "Educational Innovation: The Case of an External Innovating Organization" in this volume.

teaching and in their receptivity to lower-class life styles by using the community as a resource for learning, a source of experiences upon which curriculum content may be built. About twenty-five sessions per year were held, half of them workshops and half field trips. Teachers who enrolled in the course received in-service course credit from the Board of Education plus a $125 stipend from MFY upon completion of the required assignments, which included approximately ten papers dealing with their responses to field trips. The course was conducted by MFY social workers, with occasional guest lecturers. Emphasis was laid on what ghetto living has to offer the child as well as on what it does not offer him.

The sessions were as realistic as possible. Field trips included visits to various organizations in the community, discussions with local Puerto Rican and Negro leaders, visits to storefront churches and bodegas, home visits to students, and a trip to Harlem. The overall object was to break through the shell of limited middle-class experience in which many of the teachers lived. The course instructor noted, "We tried to have them experience, to a small degree, being a lowerclass person. I tried to expose them to persons like the homemakers who could clue them in on what it's like, rather than merely give them the viewpoint of the middle-class functionaries with whom they were likely to identify. Instead of describing migration, discrimination, minority-group status, we tried to expose them to live, primary sources who could offer vivid testimony that was hard to ignore."

The teachers taking the Lower East Side Community Course, like those involved in the Home Visiting Program, seemed to derive satisfaction and benefit from their participation. Many of them explicitly stated that the course had been unusually useful and that they felt much more capable of understanding their students as a result of having taken it. At the same time, many teachers showed considerable resistance to any significant revision of their opinions on the deficiencies of the ghetto child. Occasionally a single session or discussion, however, would rip through whole layers of defenses and permit a teacher to reach some new awareness:

> One of the teachers who was intolerant of his own ethnic group was reached when we talked about the antipathy between co-op

and project dwellers. Somehow he was moved by this discussion to give a poignant account of how he and his friends hated the people in Stuyvesant Town because the guards seemed to be there especially to ward off tenement children and to keep them from using the play equipment even when these facilities were vacant.

The attack on Mobilization in the fall of 1964 affected the teacher-education component of the School–Community Relations Program rather less than it did other activities of the social workers in the schools, such as the casework services and the Parent Education Program. However, even in the teacher-education activities suspicion and distrust on the part of the school administrative and guidance personnel were present from the outset, reaching their peak when the principals of four Lower East Side school districts sent the telegram to MFY's funding sources calling for an investigation of Mobilization.[2]

Suspension Hearing Program

The Board of Education panel which deals with district suspension hearings meets twice a week on the Lower East Side. The panel usually has three or four cases to deal with at each session. Its decisions can determine a child's whole future.[3] If he is relegated to a 600 school, the possibility of getting out again are almost nil, as is the likelihood of his learning. Although the 600 schools are reasonably progressive in intent—with small classes, a preponderance of male teachers, an interest in improved techniques—in practice they often become control camps, where the teachers do their best to discipline and manage, and have little time left for teaching. The question of what action is to be taken with a difficult child— suspension, transfer to a 600 school, expulsion—and the question of the circumstances and validity of the charges against him are charged with great importance but functionally form part of a machinelike process with which the slum child and his family are

[2] See the chapter on "Parent Education Program" in this volume for a description of events leading to this action.

[3] The legal ramifications of school suspensions are discussed in the chapter on "Administrative Law: The Case for Reform" in Vol. 4, *Justice and the Law.*

unprepared to deal. The Suspension Hearing Program was an attempt to give the child an advocate of some possible use to him.

In response to a request from the Board of Education assistant superintendent, Districts 1, 2, 3, 4, a social worker was assigned to sit in on district suspense hearings starting November 1962. This worker began acting as MFY liaison person and consultant to the Board of Education panel. As an outgrowth of that year's experience, it became evident that in order to perform the role and function at the hearings more effectively, it would be necessary to have a much more complete work-up prior to the hearings. Therefore, as of September 1963, two social workers were assigned on a half-time basis to work on the hearings.

At the point at which a child was suspended from school, the social worker assigned to the case would be notified by the board of the hearing date (generally ten days prior). The social worker then did a thorough work-up: conferences with the guidance counselor, teacher, principal, and other school personnel; a home visit to the family; contact with other social agencies involved; and brief write-up of social history. The worker would reach tentative recommendations prior to the hearing, invite other social agencies to participate in the hearing and in planning for the family, and act as liaison person at the hearing itself for the family in relation to needed follow-up to other agencies, school, etc.

The program objectives were as follows:

1. To provide continuous aid and support to the family during the period of stress.
2. To follow through on recommendations made at the hearing in relation to effecting a smooth transition into another school, connecting the family with an appropriate family agency, etc.
3. To interpret to the Board of Education panel the meaning of social-history information, cultural variations, etc.
4. To articulate the rights of the client in the situation.

Where out-of-area children were suspended, either of the two social workers sat in and served as consultant without establishing contact with the family.

In December 1963, when a social worker appeared for a hearing on an out-of-area case, his presence was questioned. He replied that he was there, as before, to help plan for the child. The assistant superintendent questioned the validity of the use of workers' time in out-of-area cases, since home visits were not made in these cases. It should be noted that this occurred at a time when the schools were beginning to feel pressures from other sections of MFY and from the community.

A meeting was arranged between the assistant superintendent and the MFY administration to discuss this incident. At the meeting the assistant superintendent raised other issues. She produced a letter from our Legal Division to the Board of Education questioning the handling of suspension hearings. The assistant superintendent felt that the social workers were treacherous in accumulating a "secret dossier" on the hearings and reporting back to the MFY Legal Division.

She wanted to discontinue use of the social workers' services immediately, then amended this decision to allow workers to remain until May. Since the assistant superintendent no longer wanted this service, it was the MFY administration's decision that services be suspended immediately. This program was therefore disbanded as of January 1964.[4]

Although this program was discontinued at the beginning of the year of attack, there was a significant aftermath. Mobilization's Legal Division brought a test case before the courts in which the suspension of a particular child was contested on the ground that the child had no advocate and that consequently due process of law was not being observed. The school board's defense was that a suspension hearing is not a legal proceeding. The testimony of the MFY social workers was crucial to the court's decision. The workers indicated that, in this case as in others they had observed, their judgments on the situations would have been diametrically opposite to those made by the suspension panel. They emphasized the child's lack of formal defense in such a situation and the significance for the child's life of the action taken by the panel. On

---

[4] MFY at this point presented a plan for a school for suspended students. The board did not accept the plan. In 1968 such a plan, called Operation Return was set up by the board. "Learning Centers." Staff Bulletin, the Public Schools of New York City, Vol. 6, No. 11 (April 29, 1968), p. 8.

February 16, 1967, a decision was handed down by the U. S. District Court of the Southern District of New York stating that a child was entitled to have legal defense present at a suspension hearing should his family request it, such defense being a lawyer or a social worker according to the wishes of the family. This decision was successfully appealed by the Board of Education,[5] but it is nonetheless true that a significant step toward the protection of children of the poor was taken as a result of the activities of individual MFY social workers in the schools.

Conclusion

Traditionally school social workers have played a variety of roles in schools, usually dependent on what other professionals were or were not there already—therapeutically oriented truant officers, psychotherapists, family caseworkers, vocational guidance counselors. MFY attempted to develop a number of other roles not usually associated with school social work, such as community organizer, in-service teacher, extension worker with parents, and child advocate or lawyer. These new roles differed from the others essentially in that they addressed themselves to changing the school system as opposed to helping students and others adjust to it.

The attempts to explicate these roles met considerable resistance. No profession readily grants another the right to control, evaluate, and change its practices and procedures. To the extent that it does, it loses its claim to professional expertise. It is likely, had the situation been reversed, that the social workers would have resisted the teachers as much as the teachers resisted them.

Professional in-fighting notwithstanding, the School–Community Relations Program clearly demonstrated the great value of closer relations between schools and their slum neighborhoods. Home visiting, neighborhood history and culture courses, and parent-education programs should be part of every school serving low-income areas.

[5] See the paper "Administrative Law: The Case for Reform" in Vol. 4, *Justice and the Law*.

13

The Reading Programs

Harold H. Weissman

The snow has been falling all day. When we go in, we will have to brush the white air off our clothes.

We made a bed in a box for our dog. That way the dog will not have to sing on the cold floor.

Mother made cookies today. When we get home, she will give us a fire full of cookies to eat.

My teacher gave me a new book. It was the best book I ever ate.

These are items from the experimental Basic Test of Reading Comprehension (BTRC) developed by Mobilization For Youth as a diagnostic tool. The test consists of more than seventy numbered passages, one to three sentences in length, arranged in paragraph form so as to simulate the normal reading exercise. Toward the end of each passage, a word has been inserted which spoils the meaning. The pupils are instructed to find the word and cross it out. It may be inferred from a correct response that the pupil was able to comprehend the meaning of the passage.

Some of the passages have an inadvertent, rather pretty, surrealist quality. But the slum child cannot afford to recognize a poetic analogy between "white air" and "snow." He must first be aware that the use of these words in this way is illogical. If he cannot comprehend conventional grammar and meaning, he cannot read, and in our society the penalties for those so handicapped are severe. Doors close, opportunities diminish, and the process of intellectual development is inhibited.

The typical middle-class child learns to read as a matter of course. The slum child, likely to come from a home in which there are no books and little other verbal or intellectual stimulation, is often unprepared for learning and may not automatically accept the need for literacy. But the ability to read remains central to the learning experience, vital to all but the lowest-level jobs in American society. This paper is a report on a number of Mobilization programs designed to improve the reading skills of slum children. Because it is basically a recital of facts, the human content of the program may sometimes drop out of sight. But it should not be forgotten that much human anguish, the up- or downturn of a life, may be intimately related to a child's ability or inability to read.

The Elementary-School Reading Clinic

The Elementary Reading Clinic began operating in the fall of 1963 in P.S. 188, serving children from that school and from two other elementary schools as well. In choosing these schools, the designers of the program sought to serve the worse pockets of reading disability, particularly those with few remedial services available to them. Treatment focused on fourth-, fifth-, and sixth-grade pupils who were severely retarded in reading (one and a half to two years minimum) and who had been referred to the clinic by principals or guidance counselors.

A complete diagnosis based on silent and oral reading tests, assessment of word-analysis skills, and an informal reading inventory was made for each child upon his enrollment. The clinic was staffed by three clinicians, a psychologist, and a social worker whose services were shared with the junior-high clinic. Not more than four to six children were assigned to a clinician for any one instructional period.

The clinic serviced approximately one hundred children a year. Of seventy-six children from grades four, five, and six, who were seen semiweekly for one-hour sessions between November 1963 and May 1964, sixty-three were retested in late May. Preintervention reading levels ranged from 1.6 to 5.9. The posttest results ranged from a reading grade loss of three months to a gain of twenty months. Forty-two pupils (65 percent) showed a gain, with the median gain of eleven months. For this group, the pretest median reading level was 2.8 and the posttest level, 3.9. Of the remaining twenty-one, who made no significant progress, eight had been accepted into the program late in the school year and received minimum instruction, two had excessive absences, five had tested below the lowest level on the reading scale, and six pupils had marked difficulty in interpersonal relationships which may have affected their performance.

The clinic also undertook a pilot project to study techniques in early clinic intervention. The project evaluated the potential applicability to classroom use of the McGraw-Hill Sullivan programmed material. Eight first graders were randomly selected from sixteen children recommended by their teacher for the program. These were children who, in the teacher's judgment, might become severely retarded in reading unless there was early clinic intervention. Beginning in the second half of the first grade, twenty-eight half-hour sessions were conducted. The evaluation report, which pointed out that the program was too brief to produce conclusive results, commented as follows:

> The programmed alphabetic approach, with its immediate reward for a correct response and opportunity for reinforcement, shows promise and warrants further and more intensive use.
>
> Visual stimulation and rote recall of letters, while providing reinforcement, do not completely meet the learning needs of our population. A strong multisensory approach is needed, plus actual manipulation of wooden letters.
>
> The Alphabetic Form Board proved extremely useful in providing manipulative activities to reinforce learning. This instrument should be used in conjunction with the programmed material.
>
> A qualitative evaluation of intervention with these eight first graders seems to show that their attitude changed from noncommunicative, shy, and unresponsive to enthusiastic, verbal, and involved. Even though the project was limited in scope, it seemed evident to both the reading clinicians and the classroom teachers that the early intervention program had helped to facilitate learning.

During the school year 1964–65, the clinic served 136 pupils: 112 in grades four, five, and six, and twenty-four in the first grade. Additional materials, and techniques of instruction were designed to meet the specific needs of the pupils, and attempts were made to ascertain which methods and materials were most effective with severely retarded readers. Programmed materials such as the Mc-Graw-Hill Reading Series and the various SRA Reading Laboratories were used, as were commercially constructed phonic exercises such as "Eye and Ear Fun" and "Phonics We Use," and study-skill materials such as the Barnell-Loft skill series and the Educational Development Laboratories skill series. Various phonic approaches were tested. Many high-interest, low-vocabulary trade books with emphasis on positive ethnic identification were employed. The clinicians also created new materials and modified existing materials to meet specific diagnosed needs.

The increase in the first-grade population of the clinic from eight to twenty-four represented an attempt to investigate further aspects of early intervention which might result in greater reading readiness on the part of Mobilization-area children. At the end of the previous school year (spring 1964), all children attending kindergarten were rated by their teachers according to the teacher's prediction of their later school success. A Bender Gestalt (using Koppitz' scoring scheme for predicting reading failure) was administered to the lower half of the P.S. 188 kindergarten population. On the basis of teacher evaluation and the Bender score, twenty-four children were assigned to the clinic. Another twenty-four were chosen to serve as controls. The two groups were matched on age, sex, teacher evaluation, and Bender score.

The twenty-four children in the experimental group were divided randomly into six groups of four children each. Each group was seen three times a week for half-hour periods, at irregular hours so as to minimize the effect of time of day on their performance. The control group received no intervention. Since the classroom teachers were unaware of the identity of the control-group children, they could not single them out for special attention. The clinicians developed activities in five areas: 1) visual discrimination of colors and shapes; 2) auditory discrimination, including games and poetry; 3) language development, including both planned and spontaneous verbalization; 4) cognitive development, including observation, drawing, and use of musical instruments; and 5) developing body-image sense, including muscle and motor control, laterality and balance, awareness of parts of the body and their use, developing a sense of common action associated with the body, and verbalizations based on this developing sense.

The clinic concluded that from the experiment that "the teachers' evaluations were global and were not discriminating enough for adequate identification. If teachers' judgments are to be used as a predictive device, then they must be more discriminating in those areas which relate to learning."

Concerning the more crucial aspects of the experiment, the following analysis was made:

> Posttest scores on color, letter, and number recognition showed no difference between the experimental and control groups. They had virtually identical mean scores on nearly all of the subtests. Moreover, both groups were more deficient in conceptual skills than in word matching. . . .

> It is important to note that the reading curriculum used in this program does not break new ground in readiness instruction. . . . The innovations intended for the program were the timing, the grouping, the setting, the intensity, and the scheduling of instruction, not its content or methodology. Yet with the best features of "conventional" reading-readiness instruction, administered by a highly reputed clinician who had at her disposal a rich variety of instructional material in relaxed, uncrowded surroundings, the program failed. . . . To the extent that early intervention has *any* special value with such a population, it seems evident from this study that the familiar blueprint for readiness instruction is not the instrument in which to invest much hope, even if it is used by superior teachers. The plan used seems most impressive in that it deals systematically with cognitive skills basic to success in reading. However, it is restricted to treating the *symptoms* of early retardation (which may not vary between social classes and ethnic groups) without regard for its *etiology* (which probably does vary). In other words, the clinician took her pupils as they came, working with cognitive deficits among disadvantaged children in much the

same way she would have done with middle-class children showing the same deficits. It is possible that no single intervention program can have equal validity for both groups, even if their diagnostic profiles are similar. . . . Innovation is needed, therefore . . .
through new designs conceptualized to take into account the special
etiology of deficits in cognitive skills manifest among disadvantaged
children. This study illustrates to some extent the futility of relying
on existing instructional strategies rather than brainstorming for
new ones.

This report points to the necessity of understanding the cultural
patterns and particular influences of an area like the Lower East
Side upon its children, influences which must be identified and confronted by school personnel if the school is to fulfill its mission of
educating the young in these neighborhoods. However, many influences which militate against school achievement are often not
immediately apparent.

An evaluation of the clinic's work with pupils from grades four
to six found certain faults with the self-teaching and self-correcting
materials.

It has been found that when a child was capable of independent
activity and had an adequate attention span and self-direction, these
materials could be used for individualized instruction. However,
many of the clinic population, because of their severe reading disability, needed the support, interaction, and approbation of the
teacher. When they learned minimal word-attack skills and felt
secure enough, they could then work independently with these
materials for a limited time. . . .

For those children in the middle grades who are very deficient in
reading, the "breaking the code" or phonic approach seems to work
best. . . .

It has been noted . . . that there are some children . . . who make
little or no progress. Careful clinical observation has revealed that
for these children there appears to be a greater sensory-motor dysfunction than for the clinic population at large. . . . Experiments
are being carried out to ascertain the nature and severity of such
dysfunction.[1]

[1] See the section on Supplementary Teaching Assistance in Reading in
this chapter for a description of another technique used with this age group.

The Junior High School Reading Clinic

Although service was an intrinsic part of the Junior High School Reading Clinic, the major objective was to translate research findings into recommendations for improved teaching methods and classroom practices in an effort to reach the tremendous number of reading retardates in the MFY area. Certain characteristics and problems of the junior-high-school age group made the work of the clinic particularly critical: (1) The program and structure of junior high school are such that the major emphasis is on subject matter rather than on basic skills. (2) Peer pressures are particularly intense at this age, and there is likely to be more alienation from school than at any other time. (3) Reality is closing in. The end of schooling is in sight, either a dropping out or a successful completion of high school; the imminent need for employment and the student's fear that he might not qualify can no longer be ignored. (4) The parents of a low achiever feel particularly hopeless at this stage, aware of their child's urgent need and yet not able to help him.

The clinic opened on July 8, 1963, for a seven-week program, with a staff of six clinicians. Two hundred and forty students, referred by the schools, were scheduled to attend semiweekly sessions. Thirty-one of these students never showed up at the clinic and were dropped. Some of these youngsters had found jobs which prevented their attendance; some had moved out of the city either temporarily or permanently; a few decided not to attend the clinic for personal reasons. Another thirty-five students were dropped later because of exceedingly poor attendance. Twenty-one youngsters were added to the program when they applied, although they had not been referred by school personnel. This left a core of 195 students—81 percent of the number originally referred who attended with considerable regularity. The overall attendance averaged 91 percent.

The summer program demonstrated that the students were willing and able to avail themselves of clinic services on a regular basis. In addition, many insights were gained which served as guidelines for special projects developed during the fall program. One project which was pursued in detail was the development of a series of sequential lessons predicated on the assumption that certain problem-solving techniques are common to all subject areas, including reading. By using objects as tools for problem solving, these lessons helped many retarded readers to perceive relationships more readily. Apparently their pride was less threatened when manipulating tactile materials than when working out a solution or giving an answer that required precise verbalization. Grammar and sentence-structure lessons were included in this program, but they appeared after certain situations such as classifying and establishing categories had been worked out with Cuisenaire rods.[2]

A very important feature of this problem-solving method is the insight it gives the children into their typical modes of attack in learning situations. Not only is it easier for the pupil to perceive his own style, but it is more evident to the teacher what stages of perceiving, thinking, choosing between alternatives, planning, and taking action the child goes through.

The Junior High School Reading Clinic gave intensive service to seventy-five to a hundred reading retardees in each of the four years of its operation. In addition, the staff of the clinic conducted two pilot-study projects. One of these projects, which centered on involving the parents in the education effort conducted in the clinic, is discussed in the section on the Supplementary Teaching Assistance in Reading program. The other project, designed by one of the clinicians, consisted of further experimentation with a series of sequential lesson plans involving the use of problem-solving techniques. These lessons were used with two groups of girls whose reading-comprehension scores were significantly lower than their reading-vocabulary scores. The problem-solving techniques were studied first in game situations—dominoes, checkers, Cuisenaire rods, chess—then transferred to academic areas such as outlining, summarizing, word analyses, and grammar.

In addition to lessons devoted to comprehension skills, this same clinician designed and successfully utilized a series of programmed lessons dealing with word-attack skills. These lessons attempted to teach consonant letter sounds, short and long vowel sounds, and sight words grouped by letter combinations and their sounds.

[2] Cuisenaire rods are size-graded, color-coded wooden blocks used by the pupil to discover mathematical relationships visually.

Initial results were promising in both this and the problem-solving series, indicating that the experiments should be continued under more refined conditions.

Reading Centers and Reading Specialists

In addition to the clinics for students who were severely retarded in reading, MFY provided assistance for students who did not qualify for special treatment because their reading disabilities were relatively minor and they showed no clear evidence of behavioral, physical, or psychological difficulties. The Mobilization Reading Teachers Program was created to serve this type of pupil. Master teachers, selected from the school system's corrective reading staff, were assigned to eight elementary schools to develop special techniques and materials for the remediation of youngsters who were moderately retarded in reading, and to improve the instructional skills of large numbers of classroom teachers.

The program began in the fall of 1962. Students were selected after consultation with the school administration or teaching staff, or on the recommendation of a teacher or guidance counselor. The Mobilization reading teachers diagnosed the specific reading difficulties of each pupil, and created or assembled prepared materials to accommodate his individual needs. Remedial sessions, conducted in small groups, were scheduled for forty-minute periods, three days a week. Each student's progress was carefully watched, and many remained in remediation for as long as two years.

A reading center was established in each of the eight MFY schools to which the Mobilization reading teachers were assigned, to help classroom teachers develop new skills, techniques, and approaches to the teaching of reading. The center was equipped with a variety of reading aids—mechanical, visual, and auditory.

In the summer of 1964, 235 children referred by school personnel received remediation in hourly sessions twice a week for seven weeks. For the children who attended the summer school, this was a new learning experience. The small groups, individual instruction, and exposure to a variety of new materials all contributed to the enthusiasm which the children showed for the program. It was not unusual for children to appear in the waiting room an hour or more before their scheduled classes. Parents who brought their children to the classes also expressed regard and appreciation for the program. The summer school also was beneficial to the staff in that it produced several guidelines for remediation programs. Some of them are listed below:

Methods, Materials, and Techniques

1. Small-group phonic games were effective with children in and above the fourth grade.

2. Lower East Side children, grade four and higher, are just as capable of self-direction and pupil-team learning as middle-class youngsters.

3. For low-level motor development, five children are the maximum for a therapist. Our tentative conclusions: Five children for thirty minutes daily, plus classroom teacher follow-up, is the most feasible technique for visual-perceptual training.

4. SRA kits were an apparent success in all the grades.

5. Most of the teachers discovered the value of using pupils as "helping teachers" to teach each other.

6. Most of the teachers began to discover that individualized instruction or differentiated instruction is necessary. We do not yet know how it can be done as extensively as we would like.

7. Stern and Woolman material [3] ensure a systematic continuity of learning. That is one of the keys to the success of programmed instruction.

Behavior

1. These children *hate* tests! Something terrible seems to have happened to them relative to standardized testing.

[3] The APC-Woolman Technique is an attempt to deal with the reading problems inherent in the nonphonetic nature of the English language. The Stern Materials begin with the spoken word rather than the single letter as the basis of sound analysis. From word analysis, in which pupils learn to distinguish the component parts of words, the children move to sounding out the corresponding printed word by learning to recognize the main part at a glance and then add the endings. In a sense, this method combines both the phonic and the sight approach in teaching beginning reading.

2. Pupil attendance was charted for each teacher. A definite relationship between staff evaluation of teacher effectiveness and pupil attendance was found.

3. Giving problem youngsters responsibility has been an effective remediation for acting-out behavior.

4. Giving problem youngsters surrogate fathers has been another successful technique.

The MRTs served over 1,500 pupils a year during the four years (1962–66) of the program.

Although the role of the Mobilization reading teacher was somewhat comparable to that of the Board of Education's corrective reading teachers, there were some important differences. The Mobilization reading teachers carried a lighter pupil load in order to spend more time with teachers and to demonstrate techniques and materials that could be used in the regular classroom. They also attended weekly training sessions with the MFY reading director. The Mobilization reading teachers approach emphasized diagnosis and development of remedial materials to attack specific skill weaknesses associated with reading retardation.

The skill-station approach used by the Mobilization reading teachers was a self-directing, self-correcting teaching technique for meeting skill deficiencies, developed by the Mobilization director of reading, S. Alan Cohen. It consists of a series of exercises designed for pupils who have specific weaknesses in basic reading. It can be used in both a developmental reading program and a remediation system. Its usefulness stems from its recognition that, regardless of the degree of homogeneity in the reading-grade level of any group of readers, the specific skill pattern differs from reader to reader.

The skill-station approach emphasizes not only word-attack skills but also comprehension and study skills. One experimental technique involves simple team coaching, with three teachers at a given grade level emphasizing study skills, comprehension skills, and word-attack skills, respectively. Children are directed to one of these three skill stations, depending on the specific remediation planned for them.

Special Programs

In working with the children, the Mobilization reading teachers frequently encountered sensory-motor handicaps that hindered the students' progress. In order to determine the pervasiveness of such handicaps, the MRTs conducted experimental research among the elementary-school population, paying particular attention to visual-perceptual dysfunction. Well over 40 percent of those tested showed severe visual-perceptual problems.[4]

The Mobilization reading teachers also experimented with teaching letter sounds and helping children to understand letter blends through a step-by-step approach. In addition, Mobilization reading teachers were involved in developing remediation programs for Spanish-speaking children who did not have a sufficient listening vocabulary in English to function successfully in the conventional reading-readiness program. Readiness exercises in Spanish were designed to be handled by specially trained Spanish-speaking teaching assistants working exclusively with Puerto Rican first graders. Once they reached a predetermined level in the reading-readiness sequence, the children were transferred to English, using their newly acquired skills to break the English code.[5]

The STAR Program: Supplementary Teaching Assistance in Reading

This is a game of finding animals that live in the ocean. At the bottom of the page are three animals that live in the ocean: a starfish, a fish, and a sea horse. . . . Outline the starfish with a blue pencil. Now see how many starfish you can find in the picture at the top of the page.

[4] Cohen notes that while some children with visual-perceptual dysfunction can learn to read, we cannot expect a large number of such children to do so when they are also culturally deprived. He further suggests that since visual-perceptual functioning is basic to verbal skill, cognitive development, and intelligence, perceptual training should be one core of a preschool program for socially disadvantaged children.

[5] *The New York Times,* March 17, 1968, reported an experiment in teaching science in both English and Spanish to children from Spanish-speaking homes. The students in the bilingual program did significantly better than those taught solely in English.

These directions are from one of the teaching materials used in MFY's Supplementary Teaching Assistance in Reading Program, a home-based reading program aimed at upgrading children's literacy skills by providing parents with some systematic, practical know-how for tutoring their children after school. In the program, local residents—nonprofessionals, most of them bilingual, representing the ethnic and socio-economic makeup of the target population—were trained by a professional staff to teach parents to help their children in reading.

It was hypothesized that, if parents were given clearly structured guidelines for supplementing the school's role in the educative process, the resulting impact on their children's achievement would be significant. Parents have many more hours of direct contact with their children than do institution-based reading specialists. Some of this after-school time could be spent constructively from an educational standpoint. The problem of reaching the large numbers of depressed-area pupils who have reading difficulties might be overcome if the efforts of reading specialists could be supported by assistance from community-based nonprofessional adults. It was also anticipated that the bilingual reading aides recruited from the neighborhood could establish contact with the Spanish-speaking parents of the youngsters who constituted the largest group needing help.

The theoretical basis for the Supplementary Teaching Assistance in Reading Program was developed in 1963–64 when MFY's Elementary and Junior High School Reading Clinics held a series of five meetings in an effort to involve parents in the education of their children. Each meeting was divided into two parts—a general meeting and small classroom discussions. At the general meeting, clinic staff spoke on informal activities which parents could undertake with their children to help create a better climate for learning. These talks, given in both English and Spanish, were reinforced by visual displays, using appropriate pictures from popular magazines. After the general meeting, the parents met in small groups with their children's reading clinician, who showed them specific materials and simple techniques to suit the individual needs of each child. Each mother was asked to try out these word games, flash cards, the reading of simple stories in companion books of

Spanish and English, or any other technique which had been suggested, and report back at the next session on her child's reaction to her effort and her success in working with the child. A social worker who was part of the clinic team also spoke to the parents, interpreting their roles vis-à-vis the school, the learning situation in general, and the reading disability in particular.

Many means of encouraging attendance at the meetings were used—return postcards, listing the names of parents who attended, the one-parent-bring-a-parent technique, and the awarding of certificates of participation to parents whose child had regular attendance at the clinic. Yet because of their home problems, many parents found it impossible to maintain regular attendance. Although fifty-three (66 percent) of the eighty parents contacted attended a least one meeting, average attendance was only 35 percent.

This clinic activity yielded many clues concerning the kinds of skill parents could master and how they could be motivated to become involved in tutorial activities with their children. Using this information, the STAR Program was conceived and finally pilot-tested under controlled conditions for six months during the 1965–66 school year. In that study, reading aides offered tutoring, or helped parents to tutor, in the homes of first, third, and sixth graders, as well as junior-high-school students. Matched samples from each of these grades were used to construct two additional groups. One was brought into the Mobilization reading clinic for direct tutoring from the same professional staff which trained the reading aides. The other was used as a control group. Thus it was possible to compare indirect intervention through STAR with direct intervention in a clinic setting, as well as with conventional matched controls.

The older elementary and junior-high-school children did not show measurable change as a result of STAR. However, the first graders gained significantly on some measures that predict reading growth in the later grades. From these findings it was concluded that the Supplementary Teaching Assistance in Reading type of intervention might be an effective educational adjunct to classroom instruction in beginning reading.

Although the pilot-study report says it was difficult to determine why the program was not effective with the older children, several possible explanations are given. One is that these pupils had "deficits . . . so great that even direct remedial intervention by specialists, let alone parental involvement, could not be expected to improve their educational status." The report notes, further, that it is very difficult to involve lower-class parents to the point where they can affect their children's reading level, since they themselves are usually at a low level of literacy and since they are so overburdened by the difficulties of surviving in a deteriorating community that they have neither the time nor the energy to deal effectively with their children's school deficiencies.

As a result of the pilot-study findings, the program for 1966–67, although much expanded and more highly structured, involved only first graders and their parents. Although it was originally planned for implementation during the full school year 1966–67, the program was delayed by protracted negotiations with the Board of Education and did not begin until February 1967. During December 1966, first-grade teachers in nine elementary schools submitted the names of children who were having difficulties with reading and who probably could not be raised to a second-grade level by the end of their first year without additional help. Some 665 children were nominated, of whom 490, chosen at random, were assigned to Supplementary Teaching Assistance in Reading, ninety-six to the reading clinic, seventy-nine to a control group. Twenty-five reading aides were trained and assigned to visit the families of the children chosen for STAR, to inform the parents about the program's purpose and conditions, demonstrate the use of sample educational materials, and invite parent participation. The parents of 383 children joined the program. Those who refused to join or who dropped out after thirteen visits or fewer became a second control group.

In the home-teaching phase of the program, the reading aides made regular weekly visits of one hour to each family. In about half of the families the aides worked only with the parent, in the other half with the parent and the child. All the parents agreed, as a condition of participation, to practice the assigned materials with their children each day.

The aides received three hours a week of training and supervision from the Language Arts Department reading clinicians. They were taught to use a variety of educational materials and techniques, incorporated into a series of structured lessons which they were to bring into the homes. Aides worked an average of nineteen hours a week and taught fourteen families. The Language Arts staff periodically accompanied the aides on teaching visits.

In the large group-training sessions held weekly with all the aides, the material to be covered in the following week was gone over in advance. Possible problems in presentation were discussed by trainer and aides, and group criticism of the material was part of the session.

The lesson plans prepared for use by the aides were a series of highly structured exercises in reading readiness in the form of manuals by which the aides could teach the parents. The content was organized around three kinds of reading-readiness activity:

1. *Practice in code-breaking,* a formal introduction to the alphabet, starting with a recitation of the letter names, visual recognition of the letters, and learning letter sounds.

2. *Formal language experience,* activities centered around simple, inexpensive trade books brought into the home to encourage interest in the printed word. The parent reads the story to the child, asks prepared questions about the content, discusses the illustrations, helps to build a sight vocabulary from selected words in the story, and then moves on to other storybooks and related library activities.

3. *Visual-perceptual exercises.* These were restricted to the pencil-and-paper activities developed by Marianne Frostig and her associates. They include tests of perceptual constancy, figure-ground discrimination, discernment of position in space, and interpretations of spatial relationships.

The Supplementary Teaching Assistance in Reading Program did not maintain any contact with the regular schoolteachers of the children, but its administrators noted that teachers did express support and optimism for the program. Contact with the teachers would certainly have helped the aides do their job. It would help decrease fragmentation, for sometimes parents confuse STAR with school, or school with STAR. The general difficulties such people have are only compounded when education, like everything else, is divided into compartments.

Some of the children who participated in the 1966–67 Supplementary Teaching Assistance in Reading Program were tested during June 1967 to see whether any significant changes had occurred in their reading levels.[6] Nine scores were derived for analysis: Frostig Perceptual Quotient, Metropolitan Reading Readiness, Total Readiness, Word Meaning, Sentences, Information, Matching, Copying, and Numbers. The STAR group had the highest mean scores in all nine tests, followed in six of the tests by the reading-clinic group.[7]

Of the pupils in the STAR group, those who received direct tutoring from the aides tended to score higher on the more perceptually oriented tasks than those who benefited from the tutoring skills the aides gave their parents. However, this difference was statistically insignificant, and there was hardly any difference on tests more directly involving verbal mastery. More important is the fact that the tests on which the experimentals showed the best results reflected the content of the STAR program. Greatest differences were apparent in the Frostig Test, Matching, and Word Meaning subtests of the Metropolitan, skills emphasized in the lesson plans, whereas much less impressive scores were yielded on the Information and Sentence subtests which measure skills not emphasized in the program. These results suggest that the benefits of Supplementary Teaching Assistance in Reading were not yielded by the aide's visits per se but by the specific content transmitted by the aides. There is also some indication that STAR may have had a spillover effect on the close-in-age siblings of the target first graders. The aides reported that brothers and sisters often observed or participated in the lessons, and mothers reported the insistence of the younger children on being allowed to participate in the tutoring. Unfortunately, no systematic evaluation of this effect was made.[8]

A major problem with the program is that it took the family situation as given. For example, Ricardo really does know the

[6] Because of the short testing period before school ended and the small number of staff, only 162 retests were completed.

[7] For a full discussion of these results, see Abraham Tannenbaum, "An Evaluation of STAR: A Non-professional Tutoring Program," *The Record-Teachers College,* (February 1968), pp. 438–39.

[8] *Ibid.*

difference, according to the aide, between blue and red crayons (perhaps he even knows how to read a little), but his relationship with his mother—who must now become his teacher—is not good. Both of them know how to speak English (Mrs. R. speaks better than she does herself, comments the aide), but they will not and, given the situation as it is, perhaps cannot. So they are unable to cooperate in such a venture. Ricardo will therefore have to repeat first grade and perhaps will never learn to read at all, unless some other means of teaching him is devised. There were other Ricardos in the STAR program, some of whose mothers tried a little harder perhaps, but were hampered by having so many other children to deal with. Sometimes the aide arrived at the designated time to find a locked door and no one in sight; sometimes the parents arrived an hour late. Sometimes the material from the preceding week's lesson had completely disappeared, or the parent would maintain that the child knew his alphabet when he knew only four or five letters. Such distortion was often related to the parent's feelings of inadequacy; she may be unwilling to admit that, among other failures, she is unable to teach her child to read. Success would probably be increased by providing casework services for the more unstable families.

Although it is clear that the Supplementary Teaching Assistance in Reading experiment must be replicated if its true potential as a supplementary tool for educational remediation is to be fully understood, it is fair to conclude that there exists in low-income areas a considerable pool of talented adults who can be trained to act as remedial teachers. It also seems likely that there are special advantages in conducting tutoring and other educational activities in the home. Finally, the low-income community benefits indirectly where there is a cadre of people associated with the schools who are seen after-school hours, on weekends, and evenings, in casual and informal settings. Their presence in the community, more than anything else, may enhance the value of education for adults as well as for children.

Conclusions

The problem of reading deficiencies in the children of the Lower East Side schools still remains in 1968. If anything, it seems more complex and unyielding than it did in 1962. Mobilization reading teachers attempted to fight the problem in many ways. The number of hours of remedial assistance given is staggering. Yet lined up opposite each remedial technique there seems to be an equally formidable disability—cognitive deficiency, visual-perceptual dysfunction, emotional instability, substandard verbal environment, damaged self-image, mental retardation, etc. While Mobilization did not discover the single best method of raising reading levels, it did demonstrate that most children can be helped in reading, given sufficient time and effort.

Learning to read certainly must take place in the early grades. It is clear that as the years pass, if special help is not given, children drop further and further behind in reading ability. Perhaps what is needed is a series of sequential reading programs, somewhat in the pattern of a cafeteria line, whereby each student can be engaged with the method and techniques through which he can best learn.[9] Up to now, all too many disadvantaged children have still to be taught how to read. Efforts to find ways of doing so must be multiplied if we are successfully to educate current and future generations.

[9] Though research was not carried out on this matter, the professional judgment of many MFY reading teachers is that the amount of instruction time given to teaching *reading* (as opposed to reading-readiness trips, stories, etc.) is still a most significant variable in determining how well a child learns to read.

14

Guidance and Attendance Programs

Harold H. Weissman

The functions of the guidance counselor in today's schools have been described as threefold: administrative, advocative, and therapeutic.[1]

Examples of *administrative* functions are routing students to specific teachers or departments of the school to maintain order and discipline, handling complaints of parents, etc.

The *advocative* function is based on the counselor's support of the individual pupil's need and right to learn in the often-frustrating organizational complex of the school. The counselor presents the student's case when the student is in conflict with the school system, much as the lawyer does with his client in court.

The *therapeutic* function has its base in the counselor's attempt to help the pupil explore and understand the world of adult demands. The primary aim here is to work through the pupil's problems so that he can better function in the school system.

Many of the activities of guidance workers stemming from these functions can create conflict and confusion. For example, when the guidance worker is trying as an administrator to maintain discipline and order, it is impossible for him to assume the nonjudgmental stance recommended for the therapist. Concerning the advocate function, it can easily be seen that fighting for the cause of the individual student can bring the counselor into direct conflict with administrators and teachers.

[1] Dan C. Lortie, "Administrator, Advocate, or Therapist?" *Harvard Educational Review*, Vol. 35 (Winter 1965).

In the Mobilization area, only a few of the elementary schools had full-time or part-time guidance teachers in 1962; the rest had to request services through the office of the district guidance coordinator.

Mobilization proposed that the elementary-school guidance and pupil-personnel services be extended to make possible the individual attention it believed was required for children with learning problems.[2] A full-time guidance counselor was appointed for each of the thirteen elementary schools in the Mobilization area lacking this position. Punitive functions were to be assigned to an assistant principal or a behavior counselor; the guidance counselors were to be relieved of all routine administrative, noncounseling functions.

By identifying youngsters in need of special assistance and directing them into remedial and enrichment programs, it was assumed that guidance could profoundly affect their educational, vocational, and social-emotional adjustment. In the view of some, the potential value of an elementary-school guidance program—if only as a lightning rod for maladjustment—could not be overestimated.

At the junior-high level the Mobilization Proposal stated that guidance should involve not only some beginning vocational counseling but also the attempt to deal with problems in learning that might be aggravated by life in a slum. This would mean using a variety of specialist services, some of which would be provided by Mobilization. Group-guidance activities were to give special attention to learning how to study, organize, outline, take an examination, and understand the assignments and demands of the teacher.[3]

[2] The guidance program was acceded to by Mobilization personnel even though it was not considered innovative. See the chapter on "Educational Innovation: The Case of an External Innovating Organization" in this volume for a discussion of the general aspects of this policy conflict.

[3] The MFY elementary and junior-high guidance counselors served approximately 1,500 children each school year. These statistics are based on those for whom intake sheets were filled out. The actual number was considerably higher, especially on the junior-high level, where counselors saw every ninth-grade student at least once. MFY provided additional telephone and secretarial assistance to the regular Board of Education junior-high guidance counselors in return for their cooperation in the program.

The Duties of the Counselor

The wide range of tasks performed by the MFY guidance counselors (noted in Table I) reflects the imprecision of notions among administrators, teachers, and guidance personnel as to just what the counselor is supposed to do. Essentially, many of the counselors described their function as that of resource persons, which, in a school, means someone who knows how to make a psychiatric referral, how to stop a fight in the playground, or how to secure an after-school tutor. One described his function as that of "making the school go for the garden-variety disturbed kid."

TABLE I   ONE COUNSELOR'S TASKS—SIX-MONTH PERIOD

Tasks

Interviews with children	623
Interviews with parents	205
Home visits	4
Conferences with teachers on problems of individual children	235
Conferences with other personnel workers (clinical, attendance, health, speech, reading, etc.)	84
Conferences with staff of community agencies	71
Referrals made to agencies (including MFY)	261
Referrals made to after-school tutorial programs (including the MFY Homework Helper Program)	85
Individual cumulative records screened	600
Demonstration group-guidance lessons given	8
Small groups conducted (fifth-grade underachievers)	3
Parent workshops conducted	3
Teacher workshop sessions	4

According to this table, the counselor spends most of his time interviewing children and parents, conferring with teachers, making referrals, and screening cumulative records. Interestingly, the table does not note any contact between the counselor and the school's administration or the local or district guidance coordinator. Since the table represents about 120 working days (and about five working hours per day), the problems of providing sustained individual attention to students are obvious.

According to counselors, most of their daily routine is taken up with handling referrals from classroom teachers. The teacher spots a child with a particular problem (usually behavioral) who needs more attention than she has time to provide; she refers the child to the guidance counselor, together (it is hoped) with written anecdotal material on the child's problem and whatever insights she might have about the child's personality or home life. The guidance counselor examines the materials, talks with the child and in some cases the parents, the principal, or officials of an outside agency. The counselor may decide that the child needs psychological or academic-achievement tests, or that it would be best to assign the child to another teacher on the same grade level because of personality factors, or that the child should be transferred to a 600 school, where he would presumably receive more direct attention. Often children who see the guidance counselor need a little tender loving care which the teacher cannot provide, either because she has failed to diagnose the causes of the child's behavior or because the size of her class does not permit individual attention. It becomes the task of the counselor to provide the attention needed.

The guidance counselor also spends a good deal of time shuttling between the principal and the teachers, and between the school and groups that attempt to provide adjunct services to the pupils. The counselor is often in a position to ease the burden of classroom teachers because the principal regards him as a neutral party—that is, not just a lobbyist for the teachers. In this capacity, counselors have helped bring about reductions in class sizes, earmarked teaching aides—student teachers, reading specialists, etc.—for particular teachers, etc. Counselors also noted that at times they are used by the principal to inform teachers informally about his appraisal of their work.

One of the major problems brought to light by the Mobilization guidance program (in addition to the strain among the roles of therapist, administrator, and advocate) is the fact that not all guidance counselors are trained; some are merely teachers who have been given the job of guidance counselor without special training for the position. What the Mobilization guidance counselors did in these circumstances was dependent on their own perception of what a guidance counselor should do, what the principal of the school they were assigned to wanted them to do, what the teachers would let them do or felt they should do, and, finally, what the Board of Education, through the guidance supervisors, expected them to do.

One guidance counselor described her office as Grand Central Station; it was always full of parents or teachers and constant noise. Another said her office was a refuge for kids who were having trouble with teachers and perhaps also for teachers who were having trouble with kids. A great deal of the guidance counselor's work, as noted, is administrative: attesting to the fact that children should be promoted, checking attendance records, arranging for transfers from classes or schools. But it was the counselor's relationship to the problem of school discipline that brought out some of the more significant concomitants of MFY's counseling program.

The Counselor, Discipline, and Equilibrium

In some schools, the assistant principal takes care of disciplinary problems, and the guidance counselor handles problems which are deemed to be of psychological or emotional in nature. Some of the counselors felt that to be forced to supervise disciplinary actions would ruin any possibility of setting up therapeutic relationships with the youngsters.

One guidance counselor described his role as the students' representative—a child advocate in the school, the man in the middle, standing with the child between the teaching staff and the administration. A teacher well knows that if she gets a reputation as someone who cannot handle her classes, she will be classified by the principal as a poor teacher, which may not be the case. Some teachers are therefore hesitant to send children to the office too often. They prefer to send the child to the guidance counselor, especially if the guidance counselor is someone they can trust— that is, someone who will not complain about them to the principal.

On the other hand, the guidance counselor is regarded with suspicion by some teachers. When a child who is misbehaving is sent to the guidance counselor, the child may stay for an hour or two, then come back to the classroom and repeat his behavior. The guidance counselor may believe the child to have deep psychological problems; he may even refer the child to an outside agency for the necessary help. But if the counselor is not in a position to aid the child immediately, the child must go back to the classroom, and the teacher is still burdened with the problem. At this point some teachers wonder just why the counselor is on the payroll.

The real difficulty, according to one of the guidance counselors, is that most of the problems are not amenable to immediate solution. Thus, it soon becomes very clear to a guidance counselor that, if he wants to be effective, he must gain the trust of the teacher, he must make the teacher feel that he is interested in the children and interested in helping the teacher. In addition, the counselor is a human being and wants to be liked. In the face of the hostility of the teachers, muted or overt, some counselors feel that the best way to gain trust or at least tolerance from the teachers is to do things for them. Possibly the guidance counselor intervenes for the teachers with the principal, or he lets his office be used as a dumping ground when a teacher is just not up to dealing with a particular child or problem, or he merely tries to get along with the teachers.

A bargain is struck: "If you go along with me, I'll go along with you" in this admittedly difficult situation. One of the consequences of this exchange is that it diminishes conflict in the school and thus keeps the system in equilibrium. A more negative consequence, at least in some cases, is the fact that the productivity of guidance counselors may be wasted. The desire for equilibrium and less tension may obscure the crucial point, which is not whether everybody on the faculty is getting along well but what happens to the child.

The Role of the Counselor

The idea that the counselor can best serve a therapeutic function conflicts with the experience of Mobilization For Youth in the schools of the Lower East Side. Counselors do not have the training necessary to give psychotherapy; even if they did, the crowded conditions of the schools would probably make it impossible for more than a few pupils to receive such service. Finally, such a counseling role suggests only that the students must adapt to the system.

The counselor-as-administrator would be required to support the administration status quo and, having low status in the school-administrative hierarchy, would possess few resources to modify its negative aspects. The Mobilization experience would seem to indicate that the counselor is of most use when he is regarded by teachers as a trustworthy specialist somewhat apart from the formal administrators of the school.

As primarily an advocate of the child's right to learn, however, the guidance counselor is in a difficult position. To focus the most appropriate resources of the school for the best development of the pupil, and to make the pupil and his family aware of the best options toward progress from the pupil's point of view, the counselor-as-advocate inevitably comes into conflict periodically with teachers and administration. In such conflicts the power of the administration will ultimately be brought to bear. Thus the advocate role is untenable. A real advocate cannot be part of the system he is advocating against.

The role of the guidance counselor for all of these reasons is an ambiguous one. Perhaps the role is fundamentally unworkable in low-income schools because it assigns to one person, or group of persons, problems beyond their capacity to solve. At best they can serve a stopgap function, referring those most in need of assistance and supporting others through crises that threaten their education.

The Attendance Program

The connections between recurrent truancy and delinquency are clearly established. In Sheldon and Eleanor Glueck's study, *One Thousand Juvenile Delinquents,* children with a history of school truancy were more likely to persist in delinquent and later criminal careers than those who had no history of truancy. An MFY paper, "School Truancy: A Symptom of Delinquency," discussed some of the characteristics of repeated truancy.[4] Statements of antipathy to teachers were frequent, especially in relation to the first act of truancy. Many youngsters said that they would have truanted less if they had had better relationships with their teachers. Many of them explicitly felt that their scholastic difficulties also stemmed in large part from dislike of their teachers:

> They asserted that they learned better when they liked the teacher and learned less when they disliked the teacher.
>
> The definition of a good teacher is most frequently seen in non-scholastic terms. Interpersonal accord or discord seems more important to them than skillful presentation of academic materials.
>
> In the imagery of these youngsters, a "liked" teacher is mainly one who is kind, understanding, and concerned; secondly, one who doesn't punish; and lastly, one who gives them work they can complete successfully. Teachers are especially disliked when they punish the youngster or continually accuse him for disrupting routines.

A felt lack of somebody "kind, understanding, and concerned" in the schools seems, then, an important factor in children's truanting. A premise of a number of Mobilization programs in the schools is that the conventional services offered a child who feels he is not being understood are either not good enough or so inadequate quantitatively that the problem tends to be reduced to one of minimum control.

> The counselor recognized that the child was unable to do the the classwork and that she could not reasonably meet the demands of the teacher that she do the homework. On the other hand, the law required that she remain in school until the age of 17. Nevertheless, her restlessness and disruptive behavior in the classroom made it difficult for the teacher to perform her tasks and for those in the classroom who were interested to do any effective learning. An agreement was reached. The youngster would not be required to meet the task performance demanded of the other pupils (no homework, etc.) in return for which she would occupy herself in such a fashion as not to interfere with regular learning routines.

[4] Robert Ontell, "School Truancy: A Symptom of Delinquency" (mimeographed, New York, Mobilization For Youth, 1963).

In effect the youngster made a compact with the school counselor, a mutual nonaggression pact. . . . The subject of this particular dispensation felt that the terms of the agreement were entirely fair to both parties.

Problem children and problem families became the focus for most MFY programming in the schools, and the same children were frequently involved in a number of difficulties which might have led them to be the concern of various programs. Truanting children were commonly those who needed scholastic help, or whose families were so heavily burdened with problems that an MFY social worker's attention to the entire family seemed called for. The decision as to who would take primary interest in a particular child was sometimes arbitrary, but the numbers who could be handled by the MFY experimental services were still, of course, inadequate to the immense needs of the school and the ghetto community. The Attendance Program was supposed to deal with children whose major problem was nonattendance at school and with the antipathy to the school that was the cause of such conduct. Referrals were to be made, when necessary, to other, specialized sources of help. The program attempted both to increase the number of attendance personnel available and to change the nature of their activities somewhat.

The Operation of the Program

In the functioning of the New York City school system, attendance teachers are field workers, operating out of a district attendance office. Each worker also visits the schools in his area but, having various responsibilities, he cannot be present at any single school steadily for consultation. The MFY program assigned a separate attendance teacher to each of the five junior high schools in the area. With an office in the school, the teacher was continually available for on-the-spot service and follow-ups in the cases of absentee pupils.

Close relations were established rather quickly between the attendance teacher, who after all was a regular school department employee, and the teachers and administrators of the school.[5] The case loads for intensive long-term work were to be kept at a manageable level of from twelve to fifteen youngsters, so that the attendance teachers would have some chance of achieving results rather than merely spreading their efforts. In fact the program served approximately 550 children per school year. Though not all were served intensively, even twelve to fifteen youngsters means twelve to fifteen families and, very likely, many family problems. In addition, the MFY attendance teacher was located in the school and hence was available for unplanned and short-term contacts with students or their parents. As the attendance teachers became better known in the schools, the numbers of such contacts increased astronomically, and sometimes the case loads for intensive work would also increase beyond manageable size. An added complication stemmed from the fact that, with an MFY attendance teacher present in the school—and especially when the worker was a man, as four out of five were—some school administrative personnel would send youngsters to the MFY attendance teacher for guidance even when attendance was not an issue. Thus, the already heavy demands on the attendance teacher's time were multiplied.[6]

What the attendance teachers were able to do was pick up on truanting children almost immediately, while it took the usual Bureau of Attendance field staff as much as three weeks to check on an absentee. A key part of the school-based attendance teacher's job was the daily checking of roll books. This enabled the teacher to determine quickly whether an absence was probably due to illness or reflected a beginning or established pattern of truancy. Surprisingly, attendance teachers reported that many teachers were apathetic about recording absences accurately or initiating truancy referrals or even checking to see if a child was in school.

School attendance in the five junior high schools benefited

---

[5] The MFY attendance teachers were regular Board of Education attendance teachers who applied and were subsequently assigned to MFY for this special project. See footnote 11 in the chapter on "Overview of Educational Opportunity" in this volume for a discussion of this arrangement.

[6] Attendance teachers were in effect guidance counselors for those children whose problems manifested themselves in truancy. They counseled children, talked with parents, conferred with teachers, arranged for tutors, made referrals to social agencies, etc.

from the program. The attendance teachers unanimously recommended that similar attendance programs should focus on elementary schools, especially in low-income areas, since truancy in a junior-high-school student is often a well-ingrained pattern which should have been picked up at an earlier time.[7] The innovation in the MFY attendance program was the availability of the MFY attendance teacher for consultation and immediate action. MFY teachers tended to give much more in the way of direct service than the field-attendance teachers, and they were also useful, aside from any procedural innovations, by their mere presence, reducing the amount of work or potential work for which field-attendance teachers were responsible, freeing the field staff to work more rapidly and intensively with elementary-school pupils. Ideally, a school-attendance program should combine field as well as school-based personnel and services. The more resources that are available and approachable, closer to the onset of trouble, the greater the chance that the trouble can be dealt with before it becomes unsolvable.

[7] MFY was willing to limit the junior-high-school assignment to permit inclusion of elementary schools (part-time) on a demonstration basis. This was approved by the Board of Education's Bureau of Attendance director but was sabotaged on the local level when the district superintendent, bowing to the junior-high-school principals, insisted that any move into the elementary schools would have to involve additional funds. Since MFY had no additional funds to apply, the program remained fixed in the five junior high schools.

15

Improving the Quality of Teaching

Harold H. Weissman

One of the assumptions of the MFY Proposal was that the quality of teaching in Lower East Side schools would be significantly improved if teachers developed an understanding of the effect of lower-class life style on the learning patterns of children, were provided with better curriculum materials, and were accorded status and recognition for their work. To achieve this end, the School–Community Relations Program (discussed in another paper) sought to instruct teachers in techniques of making home visits and give them exposure to and information concerning the neighborhood, its institutions and life styles. A variety of in-service courses were also offered, and a curriculum center and consultation service were established for the development and dissemination of new curriculum materials.

In-Service Courses

From 1962 to 1966 MFY offered a series of courses for local teachers during after school hours. In 1963–64, a typical year, eleven courses were offered, as follows:

	No. Enrolled
Home and Family	24
Family and School	16
The Negro in the United States	21
The Lower East Side Community	28

Applied Mental Hygiene in the Classroom   10
Teaching Puerto Rican Children   28
Programmed Instruction in the Basic Skills   6
Introduction to Programmed Instruction   14
Evaluation in the Use of Programmed Instruction   10
Enrichment Areas in Early Childhood   35
Teaching Techniques for Early Childhood Reading
    Readiness   36

The first six of these courses sought to enhance the teacher's understanding of and responsiveness to life in the local community. The next three courses undertook to develop understanding and techniques related to the use of programmed instruction in the basic skills. The final two attempted to interpret and develop principles and techniques of early childhood education mainly in the language arts. Although the course content and titles were somewhat different from year to year, generally the courses were concerned with these three areas: the community and the culture of poverty, programmed instruction, and early childhood education.[1] Enrollment in the courses was optional, and most (but not all) participants took the course for credit toward salary increments and possible promotion.

Although data are not available to evaluate the content of the courses in terms of what the teachers learned, what was carried over to their teaching, and what effect this had on the students, certain conclusions concerning the organization and structure of such courses emerged.

In-service courses are often required for salary increments; therefore the teacher's motivation for taking a particular course may not necessarily be to improve his skill.

The majority of teachers taking such courses are women, apparently because most men in the school system have second jobs

---

[1] This latter category of classes formed the backbone of the Early Childhood and Enrichment Program. The instructor visited the enrolled teachers and assisted them in trying out in their classrooms the materials and techniques demonstrated in the early-childhood classes. In addition, Mobilization provided funds for the purchase of equipment and materials that were needed for such demonstrations in the classroom.

after school hours and thus do not have the time to take in-service courses.

It was the impression of the MFY in-service instructors that those who enrolled for the courses were the better teachers, perhaps least in need of what was offered. The major concern of teachers in the MFY courses was to get practical help which they could put to immediate use in their class.

The latent function of these courses was to reinforce the wish to be innovative in teachers enmeshed in a system that generally demanded rigidity and conformity. In this sense, in-service courses served to increase professionalism among the teachers.

In-service courses also served another latent function, as one instructor noted.

> Since teachers feel underappreciated and misunderstood, we must continue to make them feel important. Their visit to the storefront church was successful partly because of their royal-carpet welcome. Being greeted at Bellevue by the medical superintendent as well as the out-patient director was also helpful. The impact of the course, carefully planned for them with a substantial effort on the part of many persons, also contributed to our goal of increasing their status. They are more likely to feel part of the community if they have recognition and respect from it. . . . It is important to bolster and reinforce those teachers who are struggling to understand and respond to the special needs of low-income children; and I think persons can be supported by the course who otherwise might be overwhelmed by cynicism or even a sense of lack of appreciation.

In addition to the in-service courses for teachers, MFY for two years ran an internship program for graduate teachers, Project Beacon. The interns observed and taught in classrooms as well as assisting in special MFY programs such as Homework Helper, Reading Clinics, etc. Many of the interns went on to work in low-income schools. The project was discontinued in 1966 because of the desire to use the funds allocated to it for the Higher Education Program.

Curriculum Improvement

One of the assumptions with which Mobilization set out to improve the schools in its area was that academic retardation among culturally deprived children could be reversed by revising curriculum content in accordance with the life styles and backgrounds of the children. On a simple level, Dick and Jane might be pictured on a city street instead of on grandmother's farm or on a well-manicured lawn in front of a suburban home. On a more complex level, content and techniques of presenting the various subject areas would have to be modified.

Early in 1963 a curriculum center was established at MFY. The center contained a library of curriculum materials and produced a monthly newsletter sent to approximately 1,500 teachers in the area schools. The newsletter reported on innovations in teaching practices and materials from other projects, and provided samples, bibliographies, or leads to various sources. Its regular features included news from the local schools, a how-I-do-it section in which teachers described their own practices, an audio-visual and educator's bookshelf feature, and articles by staff members of a local school as well as MFY staff. Each month a selection of free reprints, supplementary materials, etc., was offered. The center also maintained a full-time curriculum resource worker for personal or telephone consultation with teachers on materials and methods. It also provided a rapid reproduction service for material devised or adapted by local teachers.

A major aspect of the curriculum center was the curriculum consultation service, staffed by a supervisor and six teachers, each with a record of highly successful teaching in poverty-area schools as well as some graduate training in curriculum development. Activities varied widely from school to school, from time to time, and from teacher to teacher. Help was given in lesson planning and in adapting materials for the need of special classes, as well as demonstration lessons in the use of the materials.

One of the most critical factors affecting the value of the curriculum-improvement teachers was the amount of free time teachers had available for working with the curriculum-improvement teachers. The amount of time available was up to the principals alone. If a principal wished to use the teachers for other purposes, they could not then use the services of the curriculum-improvement teachers. This same problem of course occurred in relation to other specialists.

More subtle structural factors also intervened. In one school some of the more experienced teachers were reluctant to use the curriculum-improvement teachers openly, although they requested confidential visits. In this school the curriculum-improvement teachers were viewed as supervisors, initially as links to the principal and thus arms of administration—the same administration that the teachers were anxious to conceal certain facts from.[2] In a typical year, 1964–65, curriculum-improvement teachers spent a total of 746 staff days in twelve pilot schools. During this period 2,856 individual conferences were reported, which included 194 different teachers. This is about 31 percent of the class teachers of the twelve schools.

In addition to offering teachers assistance through the curriculum-improvement teachers, MFY set up a specific unit for preparing new curriculum materials. A staff of educational writers and researchers prepared and published a wide variety of materials: *Juan Bobo,* a primer in reading; *Cantamos Juntos,* a collection of songs known by Puerto Rican parents and children; *Come for a Walk,* a film strip and teaching program for language-arts development, *A Teacher's Guide to Puerto Rican Books,* and a revision of elementary-school science reading units on energy. The essential aim of the unit was to produce material that related the life experiences of the children to course content. Emphasis was placed on Puerto Rican and Negro life, making the neighborhood and its history the subject for learning, and developing teachers' guides in a variety of curriculum areas. A total of thirty-five different titles was produced by this unit.

Originally the intention was to design materials as needed and requested by teachers of the local schools and by other MFY programs. The time and cost of developing such materials were clearly underestimated. It soon became quite obvious that it was impossi-

---

[2] See the chapter on "Guidance and Attendance Programs" in this volume for amplification of this phenomenon. In a school, or any bureaucracy, the role stability of lower-echelon personnel depends to a considerable extent on their ability to exercise control over surveillance. They can be expected to resist situations which make their role unstable.

ble to predict or control the contingencies involved in producing effective materials.

In 1964 another major problem began to appear in the work of the unit. The problem was one of conceptualization of purpose and procedures. In practice this problem arose from a lack of consensus over the definition of objectives. To some, curriculum improvement meant a change in courses of study—outlines of content, scope, and sequence. Others emphasized the organization and content of the texts children used. Another split was between those who felt that the sequence in which children's learning activities are presented is critical as opposed to those who emphasized the methods by which teachers seek to involve the pupils in activities intended to produce the learning of specific skills.

The lack of agreement on goals was never adequately resolved. A separate Materials Development Unit was set up outside the Curriculum Improvement Program in the fall of 1964. Its major emphasis was on the development of materials based on various theoretical formulations about the teaching of reading to low-income children. During the next two years this unit evaluated approximately one hundred types of reading materials and programs, and developed about twenty-five pieces of reading material, including a history of the Lower East Side, an early-childhood curriculum, and a manual for teaching language development, concept formation, and auditory and visual discrimination through a series of structured sequential lessons.

An unanticipated problem encountered by the Materials Development Unit was the resistance of school officials, especially among the top hierarchy of the Board of Education, to new reading programs. For example, most of the elementary-level reading materials developed or tested by the Materials Development Unit in MFY's experimental summer reading school were based on a linguistic approach to the teaching of beginning reading. This approach was consistent with successful findings at other projects in poverty pockets throughout the country. However, school specialists who make decisions about curriculum or materials adoption were not eager to try approaches different from the "experimental" or "sight" method they were used to using. The Materials Development Unit saw itself and its role in terms of innovation, of looking for new ways to deal with problems confronting the classroom teacher and pupils. The schools tended to see the Materials Development Unit as a service organization. This boiled down to a demand by certain school people that the Materials Development Unit supply the schools with "more of the same." Such a demand assumed that the present curriculum was satisfactory or needed only minor improvement or adaptation.

Positive results in terms of pupil learning were not in and of themselves a sufficient reason for the schools to accept and use effective methods and materials. Often the degree of difficulty in learning to handle new materials as well as personal prejudices affected the willingness of teachers and school officials to use these materials. For example, the Stern Structural Reading series for beginning reading was tried out in Harlem schools and was judged successful by teachers and principals working with the program. Further piloting was carried out at MFY's experimental summer school with similar results; all the teachers who evaluated it were high in their praises of the material. As a result, agreement was reached locally to test the Stern program further in a controlled experiment in a single MFY school with Puerto Rican and Negro first-grade children. However, district and central Board of Education administrators sought to curtail the experiment during the school year and forced the program's termination after the first year. Further, the Board of Education refused to approve the Stern material for use in the schools, despite evidence that it was more effective than the Basal Readers then in use in teaching beginning reading. Clearly, it was naïve for the educational researchers to assume that effective materials will stand on their own merits when school adoption is at issue.[3]

The Structure of In-Service Training

One problem which presented itself in the use of specialists such as the curriculum-improvement teachers was the relationship be-

[3] In the New York area, home base for most publishing houses, the Materials Development Unit had a significant influence on educational publishing. Visiting publishers inspected Materials Development Unit materials and contracted for some of them, discussed material development with MFY staff in terms of what their firms should be publishing, and asked for consultation from Materials Development Unit administrators.

tween teachers and specialists. When a school has many specialists, each of whom defines his role as working with all children and every teacher, an extremely complex situation results, in which each specialist, to justify his existence, must call for certain priorities of time. In an already crowded school year, it is extremely difficult for teachers to manage their time in such a way as to take full advantage of the data and ideas of the specialists.

The organizational pattern of specialists also leads to problems. Although specialists in a school are directly responsible to the principal, they are generally responsible professionally to someone outside of their assigned school. The curriculum-improvement teachers, for example, were responsible to MFY as well as to the principals. Normally, in large-city school systems, the general policy for defining the work of specialists and the problems the specialist deals with is set by specialist groups such as the District Bureau of Child Guidance. This often presents serious problems for principals, whose priority for supportive work to be done by a specialist may not reflect the priority set by an outside agency to which the specialist is responsible. In effect, then, the specialist is a person with divided loyalty. He must function effectively within a school setting, which means that he must learn to accommodate, to compromise, to modify, but without sacrificing the canons of his discipline and without violating the policies set forth by the principal to whom he is directly responsible.

Inevitably conflict also arises with teachers. Are the curriculum-improvement teachers or the classroom teachers to have the final say on the curriculum that the teachers present? There is also a subtle factor of status: Should the specialist be excused from custodial functions such as lunchroom duty, hall assignment, etc., when the teacher traditionally has had both instructional and custodial functions?

In low-income schools, where there are too many students requiring individual attention, the most appropriate strategy would seem to be for specialists to work with teachers rather than with students. The teacher performs the key role in a school. Rather than act as free-wheeling entrepreneurs, the specialists could be organized into a coordinated in-service training department. Given the overwhelming number of problems that some schools have and the inadequacy of their resources, such an organization of specialists could become the in-service faculty for a number of schools. A team approach of this kind could lessen some of the strain of the principal-specialist-teacher relationship.[4]

Another issue which developed during the course of MFY's work was its conceptualization of in-service training. MFY's original plan emphasized training for teachers. Yet to do as effective a job as possible in a school, teachers are likely to need more than intellectual nourishment. Besides being committed to their tasks, teachers are also people who must earn a living and who have many other responsibilities, and there are great frustrations involved in being a teacher. Thus, staff development includes personnel practices, salary, physical setting, staff morale, job clarity as well as in-service training. No matter how effective the in-service teachers are and how excellent their curriculum is, if staff morale in a particular school is bad, or if the practices and policies of the principals are out of line with what is needed in the schools, then the in-service teaching will be to little avail.

Although it is clear that advancing the professional status of teachers is an important factor in improving a school system, it is also clear that a school cannot depend for its effectiveness solely on the individual teacher's commitment to his profession. The school must make it clear that it has certain expectations of its teachers and must devise ways of ensuring that these expectations are carried out. Seminars, city-wide conferences, and other techniques of increasing professionalism are no doubt needed and should be available to teachers for voluntary attendance, but each individual school should be so administered and structured that it, too, enhances the professionalism of its teachers.

The practical implication of this distinction is that in one case it is left to the discretion of the teacher whether he takes certain courses and improves his capacity to teach, and in the other case the school is so set up that demands are placed upon the teacher concerning his performance. In this latter case the whole atmosphere of the school would be professional in tone. This means that

[4] Some observers have suggested that priority should be given to the hiring of teacher aides who can help with many of the administrative and control tasks that deflect the teacher from using his time for instruction or from making adequate use of specialists.

in-service courses would be given during school hours by the administration of the school, probably an assistant principal, that the teachers in the school would have a hand in developing the courses and training, and, most important, that the administration would view the training not as an abstract exercise in increasing the capacity of teachers but as subject matter which teachers must assimilate and must put into effect in their jobs. Thus supervisors would evaluate teachers on their capacity to make use of the materials presented.

In-service training must be regarded as a tool of administration. It cannot be seen as something distinct from and opposite to supervision. When supervisory staff have full knowledge of what is being taught to line staff, and when principals assist in setting goals for their in-service workshops, their very participation provides support. It removes the threat that a lower level of staff may come to know more than they. In such a situation, more effective teacher performance is likely to develop, when salary increments are tied to the actual rating of a teacher's performance in the school rather than to an individual teacher's taking extracurricular courses.

Conclusions

The central problem which the Education Division of MFY constantly came up against and was unable to solve was its inability to gain clear authority and sanction from the school officialdom to carry out its innovative programs. In retrospect, the attempts to work with part of the system—to influence it from within by providing in-service courses for teachers, by providing a variety of specialists, by developing new curricular materials—overlooked the fact that each school is a microcosm of a quite complex social system. If this small system did not support and encourage the development of more competence in its teachers, then the best of efforts could only have marginal effect. Piecemeal attempts can not suffice unless the procedures and policies of the total school system—principals, supervisors, teachers, district administrators, union, etc.—are related to the effort.

16

The Homework Helper Program

Robert D. Cloward and Welton Smith

The Homework Helper Program is a system of mutual education which employs high-school students in the ghetto as paid tutors for younger elementary-school children of the neighborhood.

There are abundant antecedents for the idea of older students tutoring younger ones. In fact, in the suburbs and the more economically solvent neighborhoods of today's cities, parents of sufficient income often hire older students to tutor their under-achieving children.

The program was originally described as follows:

> High-school students from low-income families need encouragement to continue in full-time schooling. One of the causes of high-school dropout is lack of sufficient family income. A program which alleviates the financial problem of low-income high school students should encourage their remaining in school, provided other factors are also favorable.
>
> It is proposed, therefore, that high-school juniors and seniors (eleventh and twelfth graders) residing in the Mobilization area be hired for after-school employment as tutors of elementary-school pupils. Students who are selected will participate in a training program prior to meeting with the pupils whom they are to tutor. Each tutor will be assigned to work with three pupils under the supervision of a master teacher. The high-school students will meet from 3:30 to 5:30 in selected Lower East Side public schools. They will be expected to walk their pupils home at the end of each session. Their rate of payment will be $11 per week for four after-

noons' work. The master teachers will conduct regular training sessions for the high-school students each Monday during the same hours.

The purpose of the tutoring is to help and encourage elementary-school pupils in after-school centers, not to provide remedial or technical aid. It is not assumed that the high-school students either have or can acquire the skills or insights necessary for remedial tutoring. This program is aimed at providing the extra reassurance which will help elementary pupils with their basic school work.[1]

From February 1963 through June 1963, the Homework Helper Program was conducted as a pilot operation. In this period 110 high-school tutors worked with 330 elementary pupils in nine centers. The action-research program proper began with a two-week teacher-training session in November 1963 and ran through May 1964.[2] The action program alone was continued for three more years, until June 1967. In that year the Board of Education adopted the program for expanded use in school districts in the city. From its beginning in 1963 through 1966–67, the program involved 3,950 youngsters, as tutors and pupils. The following table presents pertinent data.

[1] Memorandum on Homework Helper Program (New York, Mobilization For Youth, 1963).

[2] The study of the pupils was structured as a classical experiment with random assignment of pupils to experimental and control situations. Experimental pupils were provided with tutorial assistance either one or two afternoons a week. Control pupils received no tutorial services. Both groups were tested at the begininng of the program and five months later.

In certain centers differences in exposure were obtained by having some pupils attend the program two afternoons a week (four-hour group) and others only one afternoon a week (two-hour group).

An exhaustive analysis and description of the research are available in Robert D. Cloward, "Studies in Tutoring," *Journal of Experimental Education*, Vol. 26 (Fall 1967).

TABLE I.

Participants: 1963–67

	Feb.– *June* *1963*	*Nov.–* *June* *1963–64*	*July–* *Aug.* *1964*	*Nov.–* *June* *1964–65*	*July–* *Aug.* *1965*	*Nov.–* *June* *1965–66*	*Sept.–* *June* *1966–67*
No. of pupils	330	540	100	550	100	600	550
No. of tutors	110	240	25	250	60	250	245
No. of centers elementary	9	9	1	11	2	10	12
Jr. high						2	2
Sr. high						1	1

Recruitment of Students and Tutors

The year of research operation, which began in the fall of 1963, is illustrative of the structure and procedures of the program. The tutors were recruited through an extensive publicity campaign which included radio announcements, newspaper articles, posters, and flyers distributed to tenth- and eleventh-grade students in local and nearby academic and vocational schools. Most of the tutor applicants were residents of the project area who were attending the local academic high school. Applicants who were reported by the schools as being emotionally unstable or whose parents would not consent to their serving as tutors were eliminated from consideration.

In the early discussions about the program, school officials had advocated the establishment of relatively stringent academic requirements for tutors, in the belief that only youngsters who were themselves successful in school could serve effectively as inspirational models for low-achieving pupils. Yet it was clear that defining tutor eligibility in terms of better-than-average school achievement, or even reading achievement at or above grade level, would eliminate from further consideration a considerable number of the Negro and Puerto Rican applicants. Mobilization felt that a major vehicle for change might be the pupil's identification with his tutor as a role-model, an identification that would be greatly facilitated by ethnic pairing of pupils and tutors. Since the majority of pupils needing service were Negro or Puerto Rican, it was believed necessary to hire as many Puerto Rican and Negro tutors as possible. The eligibility requirements therefore were set at satisfactory (passing) marks in school and reading achievement no lower than three years below grade level when last tested by the schools. Nevertheless, of the 240 youngsters accepted for tutorial positions in 1963, only 19 percent were Puerto Rican and 18 percent were Negro. Another 2 percent were Oriental. The remaining 61 percent were white. Seventy percent of the tutors were girls. The grade distribution was 43 percent tenth grade, 36 percent eleventh grade, and 21 percent twelfth grade.

The pupils who received tutorial service came from a population of 2,500 fourth and fifth graders in project-area schools who were reading below grade level when last tested by the schools. A letter in both Spanish and English was sent to the parents of these youngsters explaining the program and inviting them to apply for their children. The guidance counselors in each school were asked to screen the applicants to eliminate those with serious behavioral problems, pupils classified by the school as mentally retarded, and pupils with long histories of truancy.

Over the year, 544 pupils were accepted for tutoring. The ethnic distribution was 60 percent Puerto Rican, 28 percent Negro, 9 percent white, and 3 percent Oriental. Fifty-four percent of the pupils were boys as compared to 30 percent of the tutors. Fifty-six percent were fourth-grade pupils.

Tutor Training

Before being introduced to their pupils, the tutors were given sixteen hours of training in tutorial skills (two hours a day, four afternoons a week, for two weeks). All the tutors and their master teachers met together with the program coordinator during the first week for lectures and panel discussions. During the second week, tutors met with their master teachers in the centers to which they had been assigned.

The preservice training focused on the goals of the tutorial program, the organization of the program, the duties of a tutor, the characteristics of the pupils (including the scholastic levels at which they probably would be operating), and the kinds of activity in which tutors might engage their pupils in the first few tutorial sessions.

In the weekly in-service training meetings held during the rest of the year, the master teachers attempted to familiarize the tutors with the elementary-school curriculum so that they could help pupils with homework assignments, to acquaint them with specific techniques and materials useful in teaching reading and language-arts skills, and to help them deal effectively with problems arising out of their relationships with pupils, to interpret pupil behavior, and to recognize and respond to pupil needs.

Early training sessions tended to focus principally on the development of good tutor-pupil relationships, the systematic study of the pupil, and the mechanics of tutoring. Considerable time in these early training sessions was devoted to a review of the elementary curriculum. To be of assistance to their pupils, tutors needed to know what was being taught at each grade level in the schools. Particular care was taken to see that tutors did not use methods or activities that would conflict with what was being taught in the classroom. Mathematics is a case in point. Teachers in the area were using a developmental system of mathematics instruction that was entirely foreign to the tutors. Trained in traditional arithmetic reasoning, the tutors could do little more than check homework assignments for correct answers. Thus, before tutors could really help pupils who were having difficulty completing mathematics assignments, several in-service meetings had to be devoted to training the tutors in the thought processes involved in the developmental mathematics.

Similarly, a good deal of time was devoted to teaching the tutors methods of reading instruction. Tutors were briefed on phonic skills useful in analyzing new or unfamiliar words. They were shown how to make and use flash cards to improve sight recognition of whole words as well as recognition of initial consonants, consonant blends, word endings, and vowel sounds. They were taught when and how to use commercially prepared reading materials and games. Although the master teachers made many suggestions, the emphasis was always placed on encouraging the tutors to use their own creative talents to devise interesting materials and activities for reading instruction and practice.

Throughout the year, tutors were asked to write anecdotal or narrative reports of their experience with their pupils. These reports proved invaluable to the master teachers. Not only did they provide information about the developing relationships between tutors and pupils, but they often helped to pinpoint common problems that needed to be discussed in the in-service training sessions. Here are a few examples of anecdotal reports early in the year:

November 27th:
Manuel came late and explained that his mother wanted him to go home and change his clothes before he came here. I was working with Victor, whose tutor was absent. Manuel didn't have any homework, so I gave him and Victor a spelling bee.

Manuel kept calling out the words even when it wasn't his turn. At one point he misspelled a word. When I wouldn't let him try again, he got angry and refused to spell the next word. I completely ignored him until he came over and apologized.

Then the three of us played a vowel game until it was time to go home.

December 4th:
Pamela did not have any homework so I started teaching her phonics. She knew almost all the sounds.

I asked her to tell me what time it was from the clock on the wall. Her answer was wrong by twenty minutes. So I started teaching her how to tell time. Soon she got restless, so I gave her a spell-test consisting of 10 words. She got nine of them right.

On the way home, we talked about whether she understood what I had been teaching her so far. She said she understood almost everything except how to tell time.

December 10th:
George had homework in math. He had some difficulty with sub-

traction. It took 30 minutes for him to finish his homework. Then I had him read from the *Reader's Digest* [skill text]. He answered all the questions correctly and said he liked the story.

George asked me if we could play a game. We played Scrabble until it was time to go home. He seems to like this game very much.

Most of the master teachers made it a practice to hold periodic individual conferences with their tutors. These conferences provided opportunities for master teachers to give tutors some guidance with their personal academic problems as well as with problems presented by their pupils.

On one afternoon a month, the tutors from all the centers met together with all the master teachers for a special program. Some of these meetings involved lectures or panel presentations by professional educators. Occasionally tutors were given an opportunity to demonstrate special material they had developed and discuss ways in which they could be used effectively.

The Tutorial Sessions

Tutors used the first few sessions to establish rapport with their pupils. They played games or talked. Soon pupils began to bring some of their homework assignments to the sessions, seeking their tutor's assistance. As the pupils became more confident and skilled, they began to do their assignments by themselves, consulting the tutors only if they were having difficulty. Reading and creative activities were added to the tutoring sessions. By the end of the second month the typical tutoring session consisted of thirty minutes spent on homework, thirty minutes on reading, fifteen to thirty minutes on games and recreation, and fifteen minutes for refreshments, roll taking, and other nontutorial activities. This pattern was sustained throughout the remainder of the year.

Analysis of Results

The expected outcomes of the Homework Helper Program were classified in terms of changes in pupil achievement, changes in pupil behavior, and changes in pupil attitudes and aspirations.

These data were assigned differential weights in the evaluation. Since the major expressed goal of the program was to increase pupil reading achievement, reading achievement was viewed as the major outcome variable. Because standardized tests were used in assessing reading achievement, greater confidence may be placed in the findings in the reading area than in the findings on behavioral and attitudinal changes. The evaluators took the point of view that observed changes in attitudes, aspirations, and behavior were meaningful for the purposes of evaluation only if these changes culminate in increased achievement. Thus, these data were viewed as secondary outcomes and were accepted with confidence only if they correlated with reading achievement. As will be noted below, significant improvements in reading skill were observed only in the four-hour sample. Consequently, the analysis of behaviorial and attitudinal data was restricted to comparisons among the four-hour, two-hour, and control samples.[3]

In comparing samples which differed in the extent of exposure to tutoring, one hypothesis was that pupils assigned to the program four hours a week would show greater reader improvement than pupils assigned only two hours a week, and that both groups would show greater reading improvement than control pupils. The data for the extent-of-treatment comparisons are shown in Table II. The difference of 2.52 raw-score points between the change means of the four-hour pupils and those of the control pupils was significant at the .05 level. The differences of 1.75 raw-score points between the two-hour pupils and the controls, and .77 points between the four-hour and the two-hour pupils, were not significant.

No significant differences were found in the overall comparison of experimental and control samples. However, when extent of treatment is taken into account, we find that pupils receiving the greater amount of treatment (four hours a week) made significant gains as compared to control pupils. We conclude, therefore, that tutorial assistance results in reading improvement provided that the assistance is given as often as four hours a week.

[3] Pupil reading achievement was measured on a before-and-after basis using the New York Tests of Growth in Reading, Level C, Form 1, revised (Bureau of Educational Research, Board of Education of the City of New York, 1959).

TABLE II.
Comparison by Extent of Treatment
New York Tests of Growth in Reading Level C, Form 1, Raw Scores

	N	Prestudy mean	Poststudy mean	Mean change
4-hour	100	21.31	27.41	+6.10
2-hour	73	22.89	28.22	+5.33
Controls	79	22.01	25.59	+3.58

In terms of months of reading improvement (grade equivalents), the four-hour pupils showed an average of six months' improvement in five months' time. In the same period of time the two-hour pupils showed five months' growth, and control pupils showed 3.5 months' growth.

To determine the degree to which reading improvement was a function of the pupil's sex, ethnicity, school grade, or degree of access to school programs in reading remediation,[4] a series of factorial analyses of variance was computed. In each of the analyses pupil reading improvement was not influenced by pupils' sex, ethnicity, school grade, or access to programs in reading remediation.

In making the original assignment of pupils to tutors, an attempt was made to assign pupils of like sex and ethnicity. Subsequent analysis of the reading data indicated that the sex-ethnic matching maximimized the reading gains for the Negro pupils, but had no significant effect on the Puerto Rican pupils.

The findings on the tutors were more dramatic than those on the pupils. While there were no prestudy differences between the tutors and the nontutors, after only seven months' experience in the program, the average tutor was found to be reading .7 years ahead of the average nontutor, a difference that is significant at the .01 level of probability. Thus, the teen-age tutors not only were able to provide substantive assistance to their pupils, but in doing so they greatly helped themselves.

While improvement in reading was not accompanied by correlative improvements in school achievement, this finding has reference

[4] Several thousand inquiries about the program were received, and many teachers have traveled to New York City to observe it in action.

to immediate or concurrent effects. The poststudy measure of school achievement consisted of school marks earned during the period of treatment. It is possible that the reading gains made by tutors and pupils during the program will eventually be translated into increased achievement as they progress through school. It is at least clear that serving as a tutor did not have a deleterious effect on the tutor's school achievement.

In the present study, the lack of positive findings in the area of tutor or pupil attitudes, aspirations, and social values probably was a function of the high positive attitudes and level of aspiration exhibited by the samples on the prestudy measure. Indeed, the study suggests that only youngsters who have high aspirations and positive attitudes toward education apply for jobs as tutors in the first place. Under these circumstances, we would not expect the tutorial experience to have much impact on attitudes, aspirations, or values.

Conclusions

The major findings of the present study as regards the pupils can be summarized as follows:

1. Pupils who were tutored as often as four hours a week showed significant gains in reading as compared with pupils who were not tutored. This effect was most pronounced for those pupils who initially were the most retarded in reading.

2. Pupils who were tutored only two hours a week did not show significant gains in reading as compared with pupils who were not tutored.

3. The tutorial services did not produce a measurable change in pupil school marks, school behavior ratings, or pupil attitudes and aspirations.

It is clear from the findings of this study that tenth- and eleventh-grade students, working as tutors under the supervision of experienced teachers, can produce significant gains in the reading skills of low-achieving fourth- and fifth-grade pupils in a relatively short period of time.

The findings on tutor reading gains in the study were wholly unanticipated. The tutorial program was established to provide assistance to low-achieving elementary-school children. Yet a major impact of the program was on the tutors themselves. Not only did they help their pupils read better, but they showed astonishingly high gains in their own reading skills.

One teen-ager's report on his experience in the program indicates a possible source of this gain.

I was really kind of nervous at first, you know, 'cause I'm not all that smart, but my grades are okay, I guess. But I thought, "What if I can't help this little kid?" I mean, I might not be able to show him anything. When I first saw him, he was a very shy little kid, but I liked him right off. Then when we started to get together working, he used to ask me questions, and he asked them like he was just sure I knew the answers, and I used to surprise myself, 'cause I didn't know that I really did know the answers. And when I didn't know, I knew that he wanted to know, so I would go somewhere and find out. It was nice working like that.

The finding about tutor gains raises the intriguing question of whether high-school dropouts could successfully be employed as tutors, not just to help underachieving elementary-school pupils, but to raise their own academic level as well. If so, the present findings have far-reaching implications both for remedial education and for youth employment.

17

The Higher Education Program

Henry Heifetz

> On the Lower East Side, in every ghetto throughout New York City, in every ghetto throughout the nation, hundreds of thousands of people, a whole reservoir of human talent, is being scandalously wasted. . . . This is the issue we want to address ourselves to, not only in terms of thought and understanding but in terms of concrete action—getting universities and colleges involved in the whole problem of recapturing all this talent now being wasted.[1]

In its four years of operation, MFY's Higher Education Program has enabled a small but significant number of young people from the Lower East Side to move on past high school to a level of education which would not have been available to them through more conventional channels.

Only a very small percentage of those classified as poor in the United States go on to any form of postsecondary-school education. The number on the Lower East Side approximates only 3 percent, lowest of any area in New York City. The reasons for the inability of the poor to continue their education are both financial and scholastic. The money for expensive private colleges is of course out of the question, and even local city or community colleges with little or no tuition are rarely feasible, for few poor families can afford to support a nonwage earner into his twenties. The boy or girl who embarks on advanced education in such circumstances must usually work full-time, taking courses at night and hoping that

---

[1] Taped interview with Kenneth Ludwig, director, Higher Education Program. Other quoted comments about the program are drawn from this tape.

the work of the day will not drain him of the energy to study in the evenings.

Scholarships may be available for those among the poor who do extraordinarily well in high school, but this is a very small number compared to the total population. Much more common are the intelligent boys or girls who do mediocre work in school because of the various handicaps poor youth must labor under—inferior schools, the environment of the slum, difficult family conditions, etc. At the same time, the most rapidly expanding areas of employment in the United States are those which require more complex skills and at least some postsecondary-school education.

In recognition of this problem, Mobilization issued a model proposal in 1963 to establish a Higher Education Program for poor people from the Lower East Side. In the words of the program's director:

> The original document was really rather sophisticated for that period because four years ago no one was even talking very much about higher education for the disadvantaged.[2] From the very beginning I think that the MFY program was unique in that we really thought to reach into the community and discover students who were very bright but who had done so poorly in school that even the community colleges wouldn't acept them. And also we always remained outside the eixsting institutional framework of education in the city. There were problems to this outsider's position but it left us freer in many ways.

The program went into operation in 1964. Finding universities or colleges that were willing to cooperate posed an initial difficulty. Of the ten or twelve colleges in the New York area which were canvassed, only one, the Borough of Manhattan Community College, which offers a two-year matriculation course, finally agreed. At first, however, the Borough of Manhattan Community College agreed to open up only one of its career programs, and that to only five students. The abilities and potentialities of the students who

[2] There was one other development in the city: Some people in the city university system were interested in constructing a college discovery program established to work through the institutional framework of the New York public schools.

would be sent to the college would have to be proved.

The program began with five students and a very small staff. These original students received stipends of $37.50 a week during the full academic year. In addition, the program assumed the cost of tuition, books, and other school supplies. Some tutorial help was offered, but not a great deal. Of the original group, two made it through the college with good grades and received their Associate of Arts degrees; three were eventually lost.

In 1965 all career programs in the Borough of Manhattan Community College were opened to Higher Education Program students. If their achievement is good enough, it is now possible for them to continue to a four-year B.A. degree or even into graduate work. As of this writing, the two successful members of the original five-man group in 1964 are both about to enter the graduate school of social work at New York University with substantial scholarships.

In 1965–66 the program expanded and gradually took on full-time staff, offering instructional and tutorial support in English and mathematics. With the advent of a new director in 1966, the content and outlook of the program were changed considerably. An attempt was made to create a feeling of group solidarity among the students, so that every student would have greater support in dealing with the problems and fears he faced as he moved through college. To this end, group counseling was instituted, and a full-time social worker was hired. In 1966–67 a ten-week orientation program was held with an expanded curriculum. An educational supervisor was appointed to head a small staff of full-time teachers with a larger staff of part-time tutors.

By 1967 relationships had been established with nine other colleges, although the majority of the Higher Education Program students still attended the Borough of Manhattan Community College. In the year 1967–68, a total of thirty-five students was admitted to the program,[3] much more than in any previous year. They were selected from among 187 referrals by community

[3] Participating colleges accept students for matriculation upon recommendation of the director of the Higher Education Program.

organizations, local high schools, other Mobilization divisions, and other sources.

Intake and Orientation

In 1967, intake interviews with the social-work supervisor and educational supervisor were held for each prospective student. The requirement, aside from intelligence and potential, was that the student demonstrate interest in the program as well as some capacity for long-term commitment. Each prospect was required to take a general reading test, on which a minimal range was required, and to write an essay on his reasons for wishing to enter a college program. Letters of recommendation were also used to assess potential, and a high-school transcript or equivalency certificate was necessary. Since the program was limited in funds and facilities, the first thirty-five qualified applicants were selected.

A major change from earlier years was the greatly expanded preparatory program. In 1967, this orientation program ran for five months, five days a week, from 9:00 to 5:00. Classes were held in history, philosophy, music and art, mathematics, and English. These disciplines were not used primarily for content, since most of the students would have required a much greater time to make up important deficiencies in academic knowledge. Instead the disciplines were used as vehicles for building skills in reading, comprehension, and study. An attempt was made to simulate an ideal college setting, with close student-teacher rapport and informal discussions where the students were encouraged to exchange their opinions freely. They were exposed to a variety of art experiences, taken to films and museums. Considerable emphasis was laid on building ethnic consciousness and pride, particularly in Puerto Rican and Negro achievements.[4] The classes were small, and as much individual attention as possible was given. The orientation program included mandatory group counseling.

At the end of the orientation program each student was evaluated on the basis of his classroom work and retested in math and English. He was then either judged competent to enter full-time

---

[4] Puerto Rican students have constituted 45 percent of the enrollment since the start of the program, Negro students 35 percent, whites and Orientals the remaining 20 percent.

college matriculative studies or assigned to further orientation. Of the students in the 1967–68 group, all but one, after varying periods of orientation, entered a matriculative program at a college or university.

Problems at College

The students, their orientation period completed and their formal college attendance begun, maintain steady contact with the Higher Education Program personnel. While at college, the students are required to participate in group counseling for an hour and a half a week at the Higher Education Program center and to put in a minimum of ten hours a week at the center in studies and tutorial help. The Higher Education Program offices in an MFY building now include educational equipment, a small library, study halls, and a student lounge. Staff is available from nine in the morning to nine in the evening.

The stipend for each student in the approximately three years he or she spends in the program is now about $1,500 per year, in addition to school-connected expenses which are paid by the program. On occasion, the program has also continued stipend and expenses through the summer for summer-school attendance.

Nevertheless, regular college attendance presents a number of new problems for the students. They are likely to have a history of negative, even painful experiences connected with schools and to have strong fears of failure, of prejudice against them, of authoritarianism and insensibility on the part of teachers. Moreover, the maintenance of contact with the Higher Education Program, necessary and beneficial to them in many ways, sometimes leads to an overdependency which must, eventually, be ended:

> We still have not fully broken the problem of dependency when it occurs, and these are adolescents and young adults ranging anywhere from 18 to 30 years of age. Some of these people have been out in the world working for a time, others have been in military service. Some of our students are mothers with two or three children. These are adults and being a student is, in and of itself, a kind of regressive role for them, and a role with less status in many ways than that of being a father or mother, a family provider. Even the status involved in being a gang leader offers more in some ways than that of being a student.

These young people also enter college with a great deal of residual anger. For the ghetto child, subjected throughout life to continual deprivation, insult, and actual danger, anger at the situations which oppress him is often a means of survival and a mark of strength. This anger sometimes leads to difficult situations in students' relations with teachers, who are accustomed to more temperate, middle-class reactions. Group counseling has proved its value in dealing with this and other problems of the Higher Education Program students in adjusting to the basically middle-class environment of the colleges they attend.

A final problem which should be mentioned is related to the bureaucratic structure of the colleges. The Higher Education Program has experienced frequent difficulty with restrictive and rigid administrative practices in various colleges. While the program has attempted to establish more fluid criteria for college admission, some administrators, initially at least, have been very reluctant to yield in any way on such matters, fearful of possible effects on the status of their institutions and distrustful of results.

One deals primarily with colleges by means of persuasion, and by means of performance which is one of the techniques of persuasion. We have over four years been rather successful in this. It's always very threatening, I suppose, to ask anyone to give up prerogatives, to ask the dean of admissions and the president of a university, for instance, to yield on what they normally conceive as good standards of admission, to accept on our word that a student is ready and capable by our criteria, which are really radically different from conventional criteria. But we've been able to work with this problem because the colleges have in the end been willing to work with us. And most importantly because our students have made it.

The Higher Education Program has thus far involved five groups totaling 84 people. For Groups I to III the dropout rate was 46 percent, but for groups IV and V it was only 24 percent. (This compares favorably with the rate in other similar programs such as the APEX program at NYU.) Ten of the Higher Education Program students have made the dean's list; four have won scholarships for work beyond the A.A. degree; ten have completed work for their A.A. degree; eight others already have their B.A. degree; and two have begun postgraduate work at NYU.

Conclusions

The Higher Education Program has thus far been a small one, but it has addressed itself to a major problem—the denial of higher education to bright and able young people who do not meet admission standards.

The higher-education community has basically been a community of privileged, middle-class and upper-middle-class people. Well, now the most rapidly developing manpower career areas are those in complex skills, and the college must think in terms of its responsibility to the broader community. In a marketplace that demands extremely complex skills, the poor are going to get shoved out even more than they have been in the past unless they get a chance to extend their education. Up to this point our society has not come to grips with this problem in a responsible fashion.

In order to prevent major conflict between the needs of the community and the needs of the university, programs should be developed which can to some degree satisfy both. The Higher Education Program has attempted such an approach, providing support services for bright students without sufficient conventional preparation and so maintaining the significance and value of a college education while making it potentially available to a wider spectrum of the community.

The experience of the Higher Education Program also indicates the need for a reexamination of the nature of a college education from the point of view of the disadvantaged. It may be necessary to determine what aspects of college are really part of education and what are merely vehicles for middle-class indoctrination. Most important, the program, like others of its kind, has shown that youngsters from the slums are often both interested in and capable of obtaining a higher education. Programs for educating the children of the poor can no longer be content with conventional remedial education. The need is for a new kind of higher education to meet the increasingly complex needs of a technological society.

18

Educational Innovation: The Case of an External Innovating Organization

Harold H. Weissman

Despite its heavy emphasis on extrainstructional and pupil-personnel services, the primary objective of Mobilization's educational program was not to fill gaps in a child's educational experience or to provide more of the same kinds of help offered at school. Instead, the emphasis was on educational innovation. Mobilization was mainly concerned with demonstrating new ways to improve the education of pupils in depressed areas by seeking greater understanding of their unique learning deficits, the unique strategies and materials needed to improve their school achievement, and the unique administrative logistics required to reach their vast numbers most efficiently and effectively.[1]

Most observers agree that Mobilization's efforts to innovate in the New York City school system had limited effects. This paper will attempt to analyze the reasons for this general lack of success and to develop guidelines, to the extent possible from this one case, which may prove useful to other organizations bent upon innovation in school systems.

Mobilization identified several broad substantive areas in which change was needed in the public schools. The first concerned educational technology, particularly in reading and curriculum development. The second related to a reduction of the gap between the educational system and its low-income minority-group clientele. The third was centered on the general rigidity of the educational system, its strict hierarchical ordering, and its bureaucratic defen-

[1] Abraham J. Tannenbaum, "Mobilization For Youth in New York City," (mimeographed, New York, Mobilization For Youth, May 1966), p. 1.

siveness. MFY sought to achieve changes in these areas through three basic strategies:

1. *Demonstration Tactics.* Demonstration shows the way by example. It is an assumption of this method that a proposed change in practice can be demonstrated definitively and proved effective. Knowledge and research are the primary resources required for this approach. There is the further assumption that once proved the new practice can or will be adapted to other settings.

2. *Integrative Tactics.* In an integrative strategy, the change agent works *with* the change target, solving problems, educating, and negotiating. It is an assumption of this strategy that good relationships and heightened communication will promote change.

3. *Politics or Pressure Tactics.* The use of pressure methods in a change attempt assumes basic disagreement between contending parties. Unlike horse trading or bargaining, which are integrative, this strategy implies that forces must be aligned and power brought to bear.[2]

MFY's use of each of these strategies in its four-year relationship with the New York City Board of Education is best understood in the context of the importance the MFY leadership attached to education in facilitating the attainment of overall agency goals, the receptivity of the school system to innovations and experimentations originating outside the system, and the working relationship between leadership personnel representing MFY and their counterparts in the school system.

Education in the Overall MFY Plan

Mobilization was originally conceived as a social-work project with a work-training component. Education was not then regarded as a primary focus of the project, in part because the planning group never considered education a powerful short-range instrument for social change. Some of the social scientists who developed this MFY Proposal saw the schools as fossilized institutions, thoroughly resistant to social change, at best insufficiently informed about the needs of the slum child, at worst indifferent to him. The

[2] Adapted from George Brager, "Effecting Organizational Change Through a Demonstration Project: The Case of the Schools," in Brager and Purcell, editors, *Community Action Against Poverty* (New Haven, College and University Press, 1967), pp. 115–18.

slum child's failure to achieve in school was attributed to the school's failure to teach him adequately. It was assumed that, even if an intervention strategy was sound, schools would resist it, and that the overwhelming majority of school staff were not capable of serving as agents for change.

Only at the insistence of some of the public and private funding agencies did the MFY planning group incorporate education into the Proposal. Even then, the MFY leadership never had much confidence in the agency's potential effects on the school system.

The agency hired a well-known educator to develop its educational component. Instead of starting with a number of intervention plans, he approached this task by canvassing teachers and principals in the Lower East Side regarding *their* concerns and *their* recommendations for programmatic change. In effect he served as a midwife for ideas originating at the local level. These ideas could be characterized for the most part as requests for more of the same services then being provided in the schools—e.g., more remedial-reading teachers, more reading-clinic services, more guidance counselors, more early-childhood classes and enrichment services, more attendance teachers, and more curriculum-development activities.

The agency leadership accepted these plans with little enthusiasm. Some of the administrators at MFY regarded them as quid pro quo for two educational projects they really believed in: the Homework Helper Program and the School–Community Relations Program. Thus the issue was drawn quite early: Was the agency to conduct experimentation in the schools or to provide supplementary services? The inability to resolve this issue consistently hampered all efforts to develop a new educational system or curriculum that would solve the learning problems of the slum child.

The Leadership in Education Programs

The education program at MFY consisted of a series of discrete, unrelated projects, each staffed and budgeted separately. These were regarded as cooperative programs with the Board of Education, which meant that a contract had been drawn up between the agency and the board, outlining in general terms the duties and privileges of the parties. A school program coordinator—a liaison

officer, representing the Board of Education (as well as all personnel transferred from the school system to MFY projects)—was on
the Board of Education payroll but with funds provided by MFY.
The liaison officer was housed at MFY, attended agency policy
meetings, and assumed undefined administrative control over educational staff at the agency; but his institutional identification was
with the school system.

A former principal in the local area, the liaison officer took pains
to maintain cordial relationships with his colleagues; in fact, he
regarded this status maintenance as an important part of his role
as program facilitator for MFY. As time passed, it seemed to
MFY's top administrators that he was not capitalizing on his
friendship with his colleagues to introduce innovations to the
schools but, rather, tended to ignore the importance of innovations
which his colleagues resisted.

As the project got under way, in late 1962, MFY's leadership
sensed the need for someone directly responsible to MFY who
would administer the division and represent Mobilization's educational point of view. Although the local assistant superintendent,
whom the liaison officer regarded as his administrative superior,
offered to fill this role, MFY invited a university educator to become the division chief. This created some difficult problems.
Had the agency accepted the assistant superintendent's offer, she
would have assumed the top position, with the liaison officer
serving as her administrative assistant. Instead, the assistant superintendent was resentful at having been denied the post; this resent-
ment had deadly effects on the progress of the program, since she
was the only representative of the Board of Education with whom
the agency was authorized to negotiate program implementation.

A memo from Mobilization's chief of Educational Opportunities,
dated June 10, 1963, illustrates the problem:

> When Mobilization and the school system came to terms last
> spring in a contractual agreement regarding the introduction of
> special programs for disadvantaged children and youth in the Lower
> East Side, the plans were then in sketch form. Details and strategies
> were yet to be developed. Since then, Mobilization has attempted
> to fill out the details of the program and make them operational in
> the local schools. Although the project was conceived as an ex-
> perimental effort on the Lower East Side, with system-wide impli-

cations, the Board of Education has moved out of the picture and left virtually all planning and negotiation to be worked out at the local level. There is no highly placed individual designated by the board with whom these programs can be hammered out, activated, and generalized to other depressed areas. As a result, Mobilization finds itself negotiating the introduction of new programs at various administrative levels within the local area, rather than dealing with the Board of Education directly and feeling the encouragement and push from the highest levels.

Thus the agency began its innovative efforts in the school system with a poor working relationship between its leadership and the board's.

Receptivity to Innovation

The schools' reaction to innovative ideas originating at MFY was from the outset exceedingly cautious, even distrustful. There were several reasons for this. As a rule, innovative plans—especially those originating outside the school system—are viewed with suspicion by Board of Education officials below the top bureaucratic strata, since their approval means that they would be in some measure accountable if the plan should attract criticism from colleagues, parents, or the community. This attitude might have been overcome if MFY's suggestions had had backing from local school officials. Unfortunately for Mobilization, no such grass-roots support could be enlisted, especially without the enthusiastic support of the assistant superintendent. Local teachers, supervisors, and administrators all conceded that educational failure was a serious problem in the area, but there is a wide gap between acknowledging the existence of the problem and being willing to find out whether the best possible solutions were being applied. Some school principals interpreted proposals for experimentation with new strategies as implying criticism of current practices. Others thought it improper to use school children as guinea pigs to test untried programs. In many instances the organizational structure of the school—its grouping of pupils, its scheduling of instruction, and its space facilities—made it impossible to conduct experimentation even though the principals were willing to allow it.

As we have noted, most of the local school officials felt that that Mobilization could serve the children best by underwriting an increase in existing personnel services. This meant augmenting remedial-reading, guidance, attendance, teacher-training, and curriculum-development staffs, the assumption being that schools had the know-how to solve the community's education problems, given enough practitioners to do the job. But Mobilization, on the other hand, had perceived its role as that of designing and testing new educational strategies. Thus there was a basic disagreement, which had serious ramifications.

Since there is no single person at the Board of Education headquarters with whom to discuss substantive issues regarding school programs, this is currently done on the local level through the district office. Sometimes programs become snarled in the planning stages simply because many people at the administrative and supervisory levels have to be seen and sold on the programs. For example, Mobilization's proposed design for a reading-clinic program had to be negotiated with a coordinator of school programs, the district superintendent's office, and the supervisor of reading clinics in the school system. Delays in completing negotiations for the program were caused mainly by Mobilization's inability to complete making the rounds in these offices in less than three months. Again, since Mobilization had no direct tie with a representative at headquarters, there was no recourse for getting matters speeded through. Moreover, reservations about specific points in the Mobilization program expressed by any one of the people representing the school system have been relatively binding. Such an arrangement creates all kinds of red tape, slowing the progress of the programs considerably and keeping them provincial and isolated from the mainstream of educational endeavor in the city.[3]

Another problem Mobilization faced was that of staffing its programs. It was not enough for personnel at the supervisory level to be conversant with the specialized field to which they were assigned; they also had to have imagination and experience in experimenting in their field. There were many practitioners who met the first set of qualifications but relatively few who met the second. The primary problem with staffing was that the source of supply of qualified personnel was primarily in the school system. The Board

[3] The Ungraded Primary described in the chapter on "Overview of Educational Opportunities" in this volume, was never operationalized, in part due to the above problems. The above note and historical material discussed on preceding pages are drawn from an undated memo by Abraham J. Tannenbaum, former director of the Division of Educational Opportunities.

of Education granted Mobilization the privilege of obtaining transfers of professional staff members to its project without jeopardiz-
ing their rights and status in the school system, but those who had
the necessary background often held the same cautionary attitudes
toward innovation as others in the school system.

In effect, Mobilization had no easier access to classrooms than
any other private agency (or individual) seeking to test a new
educational idea and willing to pay the extra expense required to
give the idea a fair try. All programmatic proposals had to be presented for approval by the liaison officer to a number of school
officials up and down the institutional hierarchy who had direct or
tangential interest in the problem attacked by the proposed programs.

Changes Brought About Through Demonstration

The Homework Helper Program is certainly the most outstand-
ing demonstration provided by Mobilization for the local school
system.[4] Other demonstrations were mounted in the area of helping
parents teach children to read (the Supplementary Teaching Assistance in Reading Program) as well as the School–Community
Relations and Parent Education programs. Yet the demonstration
approach was not always successful in gaining the school's cooperation. A proposal to use Spanish as a second language in the teaching of reading, for example, could not be put into effect, because
of the school system's disapproval of the idea. On the other hand,
problems connected with demonstration programs were not always
centered exclusively in the resistance, real or imagined, of school-
system personnel; some centered on MFY staff and their attitudes.
The experience with the Small Groups Program is instructive.

The Small Groups Program was essentially a group-therapy and
play program for underachieving and acting-out children. The
program was housed in the local elementary schools and was conducted during school hours. It was staffed by professionally trained
social group workers on MFY's payroll. The following remarks
about the program were made by one of the MFY group workers:

[4] The Board of Education in 1967 officially adopted the Homework
Helper Program and put it in operation throughout the New York City
school system.

In April of 1963, scarcely before the program had gotten off the ground, the decision to drop the program was announced by our supervisor. The reason given to the staff was that there were too many administrative difficulties with the program. These administrative difficulties seemed to be that the graduate social-work students could not be certified and therefore had to have a licensed teacher or certified social worker with them when they led groups. The social workers were certified but not licensed and so could not take children out on trips without being accompanied by a licensed school teacher. Another reason given was that the supervisor felt that the various school administrations were difficult to work with and that the MFY staff could not function or accomplish MFY goals within the school physically. Being in the school physically was seen as detrimental because it helped the social worker become part of the school administration.

Although there were difficulties in setting up relationships with the school personnel, these problems were not insurmountable, certainly not in every case. In my opinion, a great many problems in this program were related to a generally hostile attitude of the director of the Small Groups Program toward the schools, confused, contradictory goals, lack of direction, and MFY's failure to involve the school administrations.

There were problems in the relationship of the social group workers with both school guidance counselors and principals, since both roles were related to behavior and discipline problems. The relationship of the social group worker to the school principal is most interesting in terms of bureaucratic change. A final evaluation of the program at P.S. 177 contained the following remarks:

> The first meeting with the principal was a difficult one. This was due to the fact that the program was not defined before I went into the school. The principal did not know what the program purported to do, and he was wary and suspicious. The Two-Bridges area, in which his school is housed, is one where there are many social agencies. Since many of the children in the school were already known to assorted social services with no real change evidenced, because of the multiproblem nature of their families, the principal rightly wondered what the Small Groups Program was going to do that was so special. He was concerned with what kind of program we were going to have, what kinds of things were going to be done with the children, etc. He was quite skeptical. The only thing that he responded to was the home visiting because of the

concrete nature of it. At any rate, he instructed the guidance counselor to get referrals from the teachers immediately and said that I should work with her.

The real change in the attitude of the principal came when he had a meeting with the teachers in which they reported that a number of children in the program had improved in their classroom behavior. Many of the children were more interested and involved in school work and were functioning better in class. At that point the principal relaxed and changed his attitude. The social worker then became an integral part of the school. I feel that this is an essential in setting up a program in a host agency. In plain words, the goods have to be delivered.[5]

Demonstrations should be mounted only if groups and individuals responsible for instituting the demonstration, should it prove successful, are committed to it. Otherwise confusions and conflict will certainly develop. The demonstration of the effectiveness of new techniques will in and of itself seldom bring about the adoption of these techniques.

Results Achieved with Integrative Methods

When objectives are shared, integrative methods of change can be utilized. Information is assembled and alternatives are examined so that a mutually satisfying solution can be evolved. When there are shared objectives but differences regarding subgoals, education or persuasion is employed. Differences are then mediated by reference to the common goals. Negotiation or bargaining is an integrative strategy often employed without agreement over basic goals.[6] Many of the programs MFY contracted with the board developed out of this strategy, including the guidance, attendance, reading-teacher, and curriculum-teacher programs. When the staffs were innovative, as was the case with the reading teachers, considerable innovation was attempted in the programs. But as a whole the programs represented a concession which MFY made in exchange for

[5] The results achieved by the Homework Helper Program partly support this view. On the other hand, conditions have to be allowed to occur so that "the goods can be delivered." Because of the nature of demonstrations, errors and mistakes are to be expected, the "goods" can't always be delivered.

[6] Brager, *op. cit.*, p. 116.

the school's cooperation in developing a number of experimental programs designed primarily to improve instruction in reading.

The integrative technique for change operated best when MFY and the school system shared the same objective, as they did generally in the case of reading. Initial sharing of an objective by no means guaranteed that resistance to change would not develop. The history of Mobilization's involvement in school-suspension hearings is instructive.[7]

In response to a request from the assistant superintendent, MFY assigned a social worker to sit in on district suspension hearings starting November 1962. This worker acted as an MFY liaison person and consultant to the Board of Education panel. As an outgrowth of the 1962 experience, it became evident that in order to perform the role more effectively and to function at the hearings, it would be necessary to have a more complete work-up on the children prior to their hearings. Therefore, as of September 1963, two social workers were assigned on a half-time basis to work on the hearings.

In December of 1963, when a social worker appeared for a hearing on an out-of-area case, his presence was questioned. He replied that he was there, as before, to help plan for the child. The assistant superintendent questioned the validity of the use of the worker's time in out-of-area cases since home visits were not made in these cases. It should be noted that this occurred at a time when the schools were beginning to feel pressures from other sections of MFY and from the community (MOM, Parent Education Division, etc.).

A meeting was arranged between the assistant superintendent and MFY administration to discuss this issue. At the meeting the assistant superintendent raised other issues: the need, for example, for the worker to go to the school to get additional information about the child. At a subsequent meeting, she produced a letter from MFY's Legal Division to the Board of Education questioning the handling of suspension hearings. The assistant superintendent felt the social worker's activity was treacherous, in terms of accumulating a secret dossier on the hearings and reporting back to MFY's Legal Division. She wished to discontinue use of the social workers' services immediately, then amended this decision to allow

[7] See the chapter on "Administrative Law: The Case for Reform" in Vol. 4, *Justice and the Law,* for a discussion of the legal issues involved in school suspension.

workers to remain until May. Since the assistant superintendent no longer wanted the service, it was the administration's decision that we suspend services immediately. This program was disbanded as of January 1964.

Results Achieved Through Pressure Techniques

Thus the use of social workers at school suspension hearings, instituted through an integrative technique, was ultimately ended through the use of another technique—pressure. By the fall of 1963, MFY, disappointed with the slow results achieved by demonstration and integrative tactics, came to the conclusion that innovation in the schools could only be accomplished, if at all, through pressure. A director of the agency wrote, "A more potent resource for community change—particularly given the substance of the proposed changes—is the support of large numbers of residents. School officials are strongly sensitive to criticism and will go to great lengths to silence public argument. Their eagerness to achieve 'cooperation' leads to accommodation, and in this exists the seeds for change."

The cause célèbre of Mobilization's attempts to pressure the school system revolved around a small organization of fifteen Puerto Rican women calling themselves Mobilization Of Mothers (MOM). This group was organized by a staff member of the Community Development Division. Their original concerns were with recreation for their children. In the early fall of 1963, the group decided to call a large meeting of their friends and neighbors to discuss what they as parents could do to help their children stay in school and get a good education. They rented a local school auditorium and invited one of the local principals, among others, to speak. This particular principal, in addition to being excitable and condescending, was also quite bureaucratic in his method of operation. After much reluctance to attend the meeting because "they should join the PTA and have no real right to discuss the school outside of its formal channels," he agreed to attend. The following excerpts from notes taken at the meeting give some indication of his attitudes:

He said that he would speak briefly because "you won't understand me anyhow." He lauded the fine services that "have been given to the school by the assistant superintendent," referring to the special classes. He spent a lot of time discussing language difficulty: "Look at how hard it is for me to talk to you. Most of you don't understand what I'm saying. Imagine how difficult it is then for a teacher to handle a class full of children who can't speak English."

The Mobilization Of Mothers were quite incensed at the treatment and activities of the principal at this meeting. Their next act was to draw up a petition which read as folows: "We, the undersigned parents of P.S. 140, residents of the Lower East Side, strongly demand the immediate dismissal of [the principal] from this district because of his incompetence as an educator and principal, and because of his lack of respectful cooperation with the parent body in our earnest desire to achieve the best education for all of our children."

Subsequently the officers of Mobilization of Mothers met with the assistant superintendent. From the start the women were thrown on the defensive by the superintendent, whose forceful, authoritative manner leaves no room for dissent. She reproached the women for coming with "demands," insisting that "civilized" people strive for "cooperation" in dealing with problems. She strongly criticized their objections to the education their children were receiving, on the ground that the mothers, though no doubt competent homemakers, know nothing about educational policy or techniques. If they understood the "system," she said, they would see that the principal was completely competent, in fact "one of the finest principals in New York City," a man who had devoted his life to the service of children, and who was continually fighting the Board of Education for more privileges.

After hearing a report on the behavior of the principal at the earlier meeting, the superintendent retorted that one or two of the attending parents were "mean agitators" who made the principal lose his temper: "Mr. R. is a human being." Referring to the Mobilization Of Mothers' flyer, she accused the mothers of doing "a terrible, terrible thing." She showed them a petition signed by the teachers of P.S. 140, whom she described as "sick, hurt, disappointed, and worried" over the flyer, in which the principal was described as a "humane leader of a happily integrated group."

A few weeks later a petition signed by all the local principals and assistant principals of the Mobilization area appeared in *The New York Times*. This petition demanded the resignation of the director of action for Mobilization, accusing him of fomenting conditions injurious to the education of children. Although a formal break never did occur between Mobilization and the Board of Education, the situation deteriorated past repair. When MFY was further attacked in the late summer and fall of 1964 by other groups in the city, the agency's potential for exerting any, real influence for change on the local school system was ended. It is difficult to evaluate the actual effect of the Mobilization Of Mothers episode. The principal in question took a six-months' leave of absence but ultimately returned to the school. There certainly was no increased cooperation with MFY because of the affair. Yet it did create a climate in which the schools became more concerned with the attitude of the community residents. In addition, other community groups in other neighborhoods took up the cry of local control over schools.

Conclusion

In hindsight, it is clear that the administrative arrangement between MFY and the local schools was untenable. The degree to which individual principals operate their own fiefdoms was underestimated, as was the need to control and influence the local superintendent. MFY needed a direct liaison to the Board of Education hierarchy. It needed to have access to someone with the authority to order local school officials to carry out certain activities or, at least, to someone whom local school officials wished to please.

Short of having direct access to powerful influence at the top, MFY could have used the support of an organized community. Unfortunately, the low-income members of the community were not organized effectively, nor could Mobilization organize them in time to make use of their power. Furthermore, it is clear that demonstration, integrative, and pressure tactics cannot be used at the same time. They are probably much more effective if staggered. Probably, MFY would have served better if it had begun by developing pressure and then, after having exercised it, moved on to integrative and demonstration strategies.

Mobilization overestimated its power to induce change on the basis that it controlled funds for education programs. Although

MFY had the money (which, however, amounted to only 5 percent of the total local school budget) and the mandate from funding sources to develop experimental programs, the school system had the population—the children, teachers, and administrators who constituted the targets for experimentation. MFY and the school system were supposed to exercise equal veto power over the expenditure of funds. In point of fact, MFY rarely exercised the veto power while the school system applied it frequently. This occurred because MFY was loath to withhold funds or programs even when it felt the schools were blocking its programmatic intentions. MFY frequently had to choose between offering the kinds of service the schools wanted (rather than those that MFY planned) or none at all. The agency felt that it was wiser, more prudent, and more in the interests of the children to acquiesce. The local school system could exercise its veto power more fully since it was not constrained by the local community (since it was not organized, at least at the low-income level), the local school board (since it was relatively ineffective), the superintendent's office, or the overall city Board of Education.

The attempts to influence teachers directly, through substantive training programs and other services, had some effects on the school system. Actually, four hundred of the area's twelve hundred teachers enrolled in Mobilization classes and various MFY programs. Yet the limitations of this type of change became quite obvious in the Mobilization Of Mothers episode. Even teachers who had been highly negative about their principal became his staunch supporters when Mobilization Of Mothers demanded his ouster. Professionals tend to close ranks in the face of outside criticism, thus limiting the aid they can or will give to an external innovating organization.

It may be that Mobilization would have had better results in bringing about change in the schools had it been strictly an educational organization. The prevailing attitude of a great many of the social workers at MFY was that the teachers were the bête noire, and that their resistance could not be overcome. Such an attitude ultimately had to result in conflict or at least in a lack of positive thinking about how to overcome the resistance. This certainly was the case with some of the MFY programs. There are probably many good reasons why any institution or system should resist change; not all change is for the good. Those who wish to innovate must at least assume the responsibility of being clear about the innovations they wish to bring about. This clarity must extend to the operational level. Slogans cannot substitute for programs.[8]

While this paper has emphasized the sources of difficulty involved in innovating in the schools, a more balanced view would take note of the thousands of children whose education was furthered—and in many cases no doubt saved—by the guidance, attendence, reading, and curriculum teachers Mobilization provided for the schools. Credit should be given to the Homework Helper Program, the Supplementary Teaching Assistance in Reading Program, and the School–Community Relations Program for their successes. More emphasis should be given to the hundreds of appreciative comments made by local teachers.

But the problem of educating low-income Negro and Puerto Rican children has not been solved. The Mobilization experience offers certain clues and directions, not altogether new but somewhat more specific: a parents' association for each classroom, teacher aides hired from the neighborhood population, in-service education during school hours, using specialists to assist teachers rather than primarily to give services to children, preschool and homework-helper programs, imaginative, interesting curriculum material, concentration on the elementary school if priorities must be set, and a variety of remedial-reading programs. What is most needed in low-income schools is a spirit of innovation, a willingness to risk. This is probably best accomplished when a community is organized and has viable means of demonstrating and exercising its interests in innovation, as well as when the school system is geared toward innovation. As such, Mobilization was certainly "on target" in its educational aims.

[8] Some have speculated that Mobilization would have done better to take over one or two schools and use them as demonstration models. Instead the agency was caught in the dilemma of trying to provide service to the whole community while at the same time trying to innovate and demonstrate.

Index